Status and Power in Rural Jamaica
adds to the growing body of literature
concerned with social change in developing countries and the manner in
which nationwide changes affect rural
communities. In contrast to the pop-
ularly-held image of rural Jamaicans
living in relatively closed communities
according to the quaint folkways of
their ancestors, the study documents
the fact that the villagers are an integral part of an island-wide society. Fo-
cusing on the impact of changes in the
Jamaican educational and political systems on the village of Coco Hill, Dr.
Foner examines in human terms the effect of these island-wide developments
on the aspirations and daily lives of the
villagers. Her analysis stresses the in-
terrelationship between the local and
national status systems, and explores
the consequences of the villagers' positions in both systems for their attitudes
and behavior.

In addition to her concern with the
implications of political and educational changes for Jamaican society,
Dr. Foner suggests parallels between
Jamaica's achievements, problems, and
potential and those of other developing
Third World nations. The study high-
lights social processes that are of importance not only to specialists in
Jamaican and West Indian affairs but
to those concerned with the general
study of social change and social
stratification.

Publications of the

CENTER FOR EDUCATION IN LATIN AMERICA

INSTITUTE OF INTERNATIONAL STUDIES

Teachers College, Columbia University

Lambros Comitas

General Editor

We Wish to Be Looked Upon

A Study of the Aspirations of Youth in a Developing Society

VERA RUBIN AND MARISA ZAVALLONI

Guidelines to Problems of Education in Brazil

A Review and Selected Bibliography

MALVINA R. MCNEIL

Black Images

WILFRED G. CARTY

The Middle Beat

A Correspondent's View of Mexico, Guatemala,
and El Salvador

PAUL P. KENNEDY

Telling Tongues

Language Policy in Mexico, Colony to Nation

SHIRLEY B. HEATH

Politics and Power Structure

A Rural Community in the Dominican Republic

MALCOLM WALKER

Status and Power in Rural Jamaica

A Study of Educational and Political Change

NANCY FONER

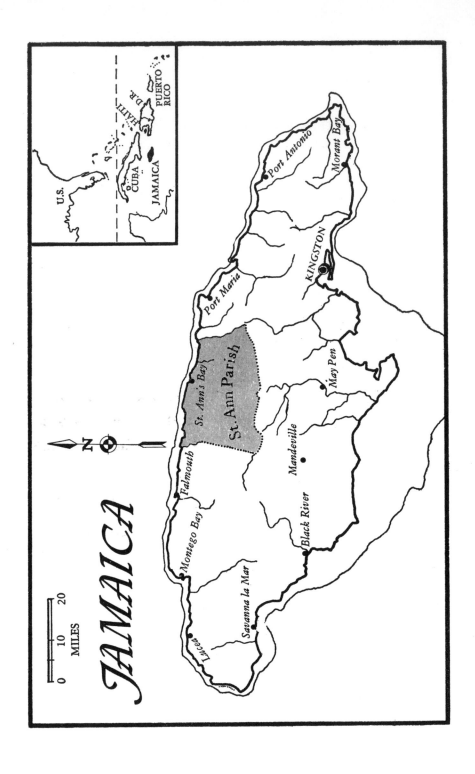

JAMAICA

MILES
0 10 20

N

U.S.

HAITI
D.R.
PUERTO
RICO

CUBA
JAMAICA

Port Antonio

Morant Bay

KINGSTON

Port Maria

St. Ann's Bay

St. Ann Parish

May Pen

Mandeville

Falmouth

Montego Bay

Black River

Savanna la Mar

Lucea

Status
and Power
in Rural
Jamaica

A Study of Educational
and Political Change

NANCY FONER

Teachers College Press
Teachers College, Columbia University
New York and London

To my Parents

Editor's Note

The study of Jamaican society and culture dates back over half a century to when Martha Warren Beckwith began doing research and writing on the people of the Jamaican countryside. In 1929, her efforts culminated in the now well-known publication *Black Roadways: A Study of Jamaican Folk Life*. Since then, particularly after World War II, scores of Jamaican, British, North American, and European anthropologists, including many of international reputation, have carried out significant research on the island, among them, Madeline Kerr, Fernando Henriques, Yehudi Cohen, Edith Clarke, George Eaton Simpson, M.G. Smith, G.J. Kruijer, Sidney W. Mintz and Orlando Patterson. Their topics and theoretical perspectives have been diverse, but, given priorities and interests of particular periods, this body of research does not present a thorough or balanced coverage of major anthropological problems in Jamaica. Education, for example, has received only minimal anthropological attention. Before this volume, little existed that focused on this sensitive and pressing subject, aside from several insightful and provocative articles by M.G. Smith and Edward Seaga. *Status and Power in Rural Jamaica* by Nancy Foner is the first full anthropological monograph with Jamaican education as its central theme. Utilizing as it does the community as the central unit of analysis, this volume may well be the first of its genre for the entire Caribbean region.

The author's original intent was to study the impact of nationhood and independence in a rural community (Jamaica shed colonial status in 1962), but she came to the realization that political change could not be dealt with without first explaining why education was of such vital importance to the villagers. As a consequence education became the dominant *leit motif* of the study and of the resultant book. In these pages, then, Dr. Foner incisively probes into the effects of national education on the local status system, on status aspirations, and on village crises and disputes. It is a study that not only has relevance to Jamaica but, I believe, to many of the ex-colonial, developing countries of the world.

This is the seventh in a series sponsored by the Center for Education in Latin America, a series which attempts to bring forth the specifics of formal education and to offer materials and analyses that place the educational process in meaningful context. Geographically, the series concentrates on those political units, nations, territories, and colonies south of the Rio Grande, commonly referred to as Latin America and the Caribbean. These constituent societies form a complex sphere that, with considerable theoretical difficulty, can be ordered into three culturally distinctive segments, a tripartite scheme that illuminates the heterogeneity of the area. Within each subdivision, uniformities in historical development, similar patterns of economic exploitation, and indigenous populations of approximately equal size and complexity have led to structurally homologous forms of social organization and articulation. Social institutions in each of these subdivisions, including those related to education, have developed distinctively regional forms and carry specific social significance.

One subdivision includes the territories and countries of the Antilles and the Circum-Caribbean. Characteristically, these societies contain institutions that bear the imprint of a long colonial heritage and a social legacy from forced connection with the metropoles of Western Europe. The populations of many of these societies have been derived primarily from Africa, but they also include important pockets of people with origins in Europe, the Indian subcontinent, China, and the Middle East. *We Wish to Be Looked Upon, Black Images, Politics and the Power Structure,* and now *Status and Power in Rural Jamaica* are books in this series that concentrate on these island and coastal polities. A second subdivision includes those countries, most often located in the highlands of South and Central America, that contain large, culturally viable populations of Amerindians and in which the process of social and cultural integration of native peoples has dramatically influenced the course and form of nationbuilding. *The Middle Beat* and *Telling Tongues* deal with nations in this subdivision, a region sometimes referred to as Indo-America. The third subdivision encompasses the societies of the southern, temperate zones of the Western Hemisphere, which demographically and culturally are dominated by the descendants of migrants from Europe. *Guidelines to Problems of Education in Brazil* focuses on this region.

Lambros Comitas

November 1972

Foreword

In the second chapter of this book Dr. Foner tells us that practically all of the people in the community of Coco Hill ranked themselves as members of the "lower class" and described themselves as being "poor." For anyone who has worked in the Caribbean this has a familiar ring—from the plantations of Guyana to the small farmers of Jamaica there is a shared feeling of "persistent poverty" as Dr. George Beckford calls it in the title of his recent book.[1]

There can be no doubt of the existence of real poverty in Jamaica, urban and rural, yet by world standards Jamaica is not a poor country and many of the people of Coco Hill who described themselves as being poor were actually fairly well-off. It seems clear that over and above the facts of absolute deprivation and uneven distribution of wealth there is a deeper meaning to the concept of "poverty" which can be understood only in the context of Jamaican and West Indian history.

Coco Hill is situated in one of the most prosperous agricultural areas of Jamaica where the growing of so-called "minor crops" such as coffee, pimento, ginger, and arrowroot had begun even before slavery was abolished in 1838. Whereas sugar had always been as-

[1] Beckford, George, *Persistent Poverty: Underdevelopment in Plantation Economies of the Third World*, Oxford University Press, 1972.

sociated with the social and political domination of a white planter class, frequently absentee, these "minor" crops were taken up and developed by Coloured and Black Jamaicans trading through an authentically Jamaican merchant class.[2] The development of the banana trade from the 1870's onward further consolidated the relative prosperity of this rural section of the Jamaican population until by 1910 bananas accounted for 52 per cent of the value of Jamaican exports while sugar had fallen to a mere 8 per cent.[3]

This rural economic complex was the foundation on which an important part of Jamaica's expanding middle and lower middle class was based. It predated bananas; in 1846 when the British discontinued their direct grants to education on the grounds that the ex-slave population of Jamaica was better able to support its own schools than was the British working class, it was this sector of the rural population, rather than the sugar workers, that was being referred to. The British argument may have been exaggerated, but the wave of prosperity which had been evident in the early 1840's left behind, as it receded, a core of small and medium farmers. That core has persisted through similar waves of prosperity and recession, continuing to be much better off than the marginal peasants who have to depend upon wage labour to make ends meet. Yet, despite this differentiation of the rural population we find a sense of uniformity of condition—of persistent poverty.

When we think of the process of "urbanisation" in Jamaica we tend to think in stereotypical terms of the movement of impoverished people into the slums of Kingston. Certainly that has been part of the reality of Jamaican experience, but there has also been a significant movement of more prosperous people, and their children, into urban white-collar occupations, particularly into teaching and the lower ranks of the civil service. It is the more recent manifestation of these trends that Dr. Foner's study documents so well, and her discussions of the symbolic value of education and escape from manual labour reveal long-standing patterns.

Professor Arthur Lewis has observed that Jamaica did not "find among her own people spokesmen whose primary concern was economic and social development."[4] He argues that prior to 1930 the Jamaican middle and upper classes were preoccupied with questions

[2] See Hall, Douglas, *Free Jamaica 1838–1865*, Yale University Press, 1959.

[3] Eisner, G., *Jamaica 1830–1930*, Manchester University Press, 1961, p. 238.

[4] Introduction to Eisner, *op. cit.*, p. xxiii.

of political power and status, and that the British Governors were frequently more enlightened than local spokesmen. It is true that local capital, much of it in the hands of Jewish and Coloured Jamaicans, was insufficiently applied to creative development of the manufacturing and local food production sectors of the economy, but the reasons for this have to be sought in the distorting effects of colonial rule rather than in some inherent lack of ability, or sheer selfishness on the part of local capitalists.

The new hierarchy imposed by Crown Colony Government after 1865 was based on a combination of race and culture. While the British disseminated an ideal of tutelary democracy and equality before the law for all men regardless of colour, it was they who set the standards for the racial calibration of the social scale. Status came to be based upon a combination of race and "refinement" which was less brutal than the overtly racial hierarchy of slave society, but it also lacked whatever entrepreneurial drive that sorry system had possessed. Thus the coalition of local labour and local capital in the development of a local economy opposed to the imperially financed sugar industry, a coalition which had found a voice in the old democratic Assembly prior to 1865, was broken—or at least severely damaged—and the "plural society" view of a *culturally* and racially divided society came to predominate.[5] It is by reference to these colonial standards of social worth that the self-evaluation of rural people as "poor" has to be understood, and that the apparent self-indulgence of the colonial middle class must be judged.

One of the most astonishing facts reported in this book is that prior to 1953 no child from Coco Hill had ever been to secondary school, and this despite the fact that a neighbouring town has long been a centre for secondary education. As Dr. Foner makes clear, colonial Jamaica simply did not encourage the children of rural Black people to aspire to secondary school entry, and there was no system of rural primary school education suitable to preparing children for such a move. The society was structured to maintain a sharp distinction between the middle class, which defined itself as Coloured and educated, and the lower class, which was defined as Black, uneducated, and perhaps so different as to be uneducable. At that level of distinction the "lower class" was regarded as being relatively undifferentiated. This middle-class image was not meant to *explain* anything (in that respect it was unlike the theory of the plural society); it was meant

[5] This point has been well made by D. Robotham, "Class Structure & Community Structure in Jamaica," Unpublished M.A. thesis, Department of Anthropology, University of Chicago, 1970.

to perpetuate a state of affairs. Of course it was as factually incorrect as it was morally repugnant; there was *some* mobility out of the rural areas—into teaching in particular. The system of training on the job through the pupil-teacher system gave many rural people of modest means an educational opportunity, and through the teaching profession a body of able people came to constitute a nucleus for future leadership.

Modern Jamaican nationalism is beginning to repair the damage done by colonial rule in damping down the ambitions and creative energies of the Jamaican Black population. Nationalism has begun to rebuild the relationship between local entrepreneurial skill and the needs of the Jamaican people but at a different, more industrialised, level. The centre of gravity of the society is no longer in the rural areas but in the growing working class areas of Kingston and the other towns. The difficulties of social and economic development are enormous, particularly in a world where it is easier to continue to depend on outside initiative, and to invite enterprise rather than display it, but there has been marked development in industry and a resurgence of local entrepreneurial effort.

What Dr. Foner's book shows us is the interaction between these modern developments and the residue of a system of social relationships continuing from the past. Although in one sense this is a "community study," its significance is not confined to what it tells us about one rural community. The processes discussed here are inherent in the changes through which Jamaica is passing, and are to be found in Kingston as well as in the country. The author never lets us forget that Coco Hill is an integral part of Jamaican society and the things that go on there are not merely particular to this place. It is because she has a theoretical framework which directs her attention to significant aspects of status interaction that she is able to display for our consideration processes which are relevant to a much wider field of social relations. Above all, she disposes of the myth of the plural society. It is difficult to see how anyone could continue to insist upon the notion of "cultural sections" characterised by differing institutions, or the idea of Jamaican rural communities as "closed," after reading this book. What she does in fact is show just how and why the concept of "pluralism" has operated in the past to maintain a class boundary which has quickly yielded to penetration as soon as the means became available. How far the change will proceed and what its eventual outcome will be is for the Jamaican people to decide, but it is remarkable to find the determination and ambition which is documented in this book.

In spite of the extent and rapidity of change, there is evidence enough of the failure to meet the expectations of large numbers of people. Jamaica is experiencing a "bourgeois" revolution, drawing ever more people into the lower levels of the "middle class" with a style of life most clearly expressed in the new housing development schemes, and their adjunct shopping centres, which are mushrooming all over the island. Inevitably, large numbers of people are left behind. As Dr. Foner shows, the primary school in Coco Hill is overcrowded and the teachers are forced to neglect some children. It is not surprising that they concentrate their attention on those whose parents are known to have the means and the ambition to encourage their children to do well and go on to higher education. Thus a vicious circle is set up, and while the "poor" are not yet a segregated minority as in the United States, the dynamic of the present system certainly tends in that direction.

In a small community such as Coco Hill there is sufficient intimacy, face-to-face contact and kinship connection to ensure that relations are kept at the level of interpersonal dispute, spite, and envy even when people are growing apart in terms of their social status. If children of a particular family are accused of being less bright than others and it is asserted that they cannot "pass exam," this results in "fuss" of a limited nature. Once the poor become segregated, either as a result of racial bigotry or as a consequence of urban concentration, it does not take long for academics of limited sensibility to begin developing theories about the genetic inferiority of the poor. Such theories are a projection at a new and more dangerous level of the same self-justifying ideas we see here on a more modest scale. With urban segregation the "poor" become a category and are no longer experienced as real human beings.

It is a measure of the relevance of Dr. Foner's work that it should raise such questions. While the reader will be delighted by the humanity of the actors in this story and often moved by their heroic efforts on behalf of their children, he will also be reminded that "progress" of the kind being experienced here exacts enormous social costs.

Raymond T. Smith
Chicago, Illinois, 1972

Acknowledgements

This study is based on fieldwork in the rural Jamaican community of Coco Hill (a pseudonym), in which I lived from July 1968 through September 1969. The study could not have been carried out or written without the aid of numerous people. My greatest debt is to Raymond T. Smith who supervised my graduate studies at the University of Chicago, helped me to select a field site, and provided me with initial field training. Without his encouragement, patience, criticism, and advice this book could not have been completed.

In addition, I am grateful to many members of the faculty of the University of the West Indies, in particular, Lloyd Braithwaite (now Pro-Vice-Chancellor, University of the West Indies, St. Augustine, Trinidad) and Robin Mackenzie (now at Macquarie University). They provided helpful comments on my research and were always ready to go out of their way to help with any problems I had while I was in Jamaica. The Institute of Social and Economic Research, University of the West Indies also made its extensive library available to me.

My thanks go also to those who read the manuscript, in various stages of preparation, and who made valuable comments which helped in its completion: Bernard Cohn; Lambros Comitas; Lloyd Fallers; Patricia Lander; Vera Rubin. I am deeply grateful to my mother, Anne Foner, of the Department of Sociology, Rutgers University, for making detailed constructive criticisms and helping me to prepare the manuscript for publication.

I also wish to thank the various agencies which supported my research: National Defense Education Act Title IV fellowship, summer 1968; National Institute of Mental Health, Public Health Service fellowship, October 1968 to October 1970, and field training grant, October 1968 to October 1969.

I am indebted, above all, to the villagers of Coco Hill, who must remain anonymous. Throughout the book I have used fictitious names and have tried to conceal the identities of those persons mentioned. The villagers not only provided the information on which this study is based, but extended to me their friendship, trust, and encouragement. For just as they are anxious for their own children to "get on," the villagers helped me to carry on my research, since they felt it was important for me to "get on" and to complete my academic training. While I have succeeded in this aim, most of the villagers and their children have not been so fortunate. In fact, villagers often asked whether my research would help them in any way, and I would have to tell them regretfully that this was quite unlikely. The solutions to the problems which Jamaica faces and which block the villagers' changes to attain their goals cannot be provided by an anthropological study. My hope is, however, that this book will contribute to an understanding of the life of rural Jamaicans and the difficulties that they confront and, in some small way, aid in the eventual improvement of their lives.

N.F.
New York, 1972

Contents

Introduction

One of the things most striking to a visitor in rural Jamaica is the enthusiasm the villagers have for education. When I came to the village of Coco Hill, I did not expect that education would be so central to the lives of the villagers. My original interest had been in the impact of nationhood and independence on a rural community. I intended to concentrate my attention on local branches of political parties and other new nationwide associations, and on interpersonal relations as they concerned political processes. However, as so often happens, preconceptions of what would be meaningful to the people involved were not correct. It was not that I had failed to recognize that education was an important aspect of the modernization process, but I had relegated educational expansion to the "of course" category of events. It took me only a few months to realize that if I were to describe and explain accurately the impact of political changes on rural Jamaican life, I would have to explore just why education was so significant. This study, then, is the outcome of one outside observer's attempt to understand the impact of Jamaica's expanded educational system and new national political structure on the lives of ordinary people in one small rural community.

A rural community in Jamaica—no matter how isolated it seems

—is very much a part of the whole society. The social life of a small community must be pictured against the background of the larger social structure and the changes that have occurred on the whole island. The most dramatic recent change in Jamaica has been the granting of independence by Great Britain in 1962, but as Joseph Schumpeter has noted, "Every social situation is the heritage of preceding situations." [1] Even before independence there had been a transformation in the political life of the island. Constitutional reforms in the early 1940's instituted universal adult suffrage, and political parties and their trade union affiliates were formed at that time. Since independence there have been two noteworthy changes: Jamaicans now occupy most of the highest political and administrative posts on the island, and the ideological basis of politics has shifted. Under British rule, the notion that people should be judged and allocated to social positions in Jamaica on the basis of merit had already been institutionalized, but it was the English who held the top positions in the various administrative hierarchies and who, through informal means, restricted access to education, the major channel of upward mobility. Present political leaders in Jamaica, as in other new states, claim that they are equalizing access to achievement. To this end they have organized development and welfare programs and, most important, they are expanding educational opportunities so that chances to compete in the educational system are more widely available.

The government's role in economic development, in contrast, has been rather limited; it has largely confined itself to providing incentives for private Jamaican and international companies. However, the general nature of the economy has changed. Since the end of World War II, there has been a rise in Jamaica's national income and living standards, from increased receipts for the export of bauxite, agricultural products, some manufactured goods, and the developing tourist industry. There has been growth in the construction and in light consumer goods industries, although a large proportion of both manufactured goods and food are still imported. These developments have given rise to a new elite in business, construction, and commerce and have provided new jobs at lower levels of the occupational system. Tied to Britain through preferential trade agreements for bananas and sugar, Jamaica is developing closer ties based on bauxite, manufacturing,* and tourism with the United States and Canada. Gordon Lewis, discussing Puerto Rico, sums up Jamaica's situation quite well:

There has been taking place, in fact, a very real structural trans-

---

* This manufacturing is mainly conducted by American companies who use the cheaper and more abundant Jamaican labor force for such processes as stitching brassieres and making cheap jewelry and clothing.

formation of the economy and its work structure . . . . The capital basis is shifting from the ownership of land to industrial, bureaucratic, and commercial activity as preferred styles of economic activity.[2]

An increased proportion of the labor force is engaged in non-agricultural activities, such as skilled and industrial occupations, transportation, communications, construction, and mining.* There has also been a shift from individual to corporate ownership of plantations and the development of a new urban middle class, oriented to consumption and the emulation of an American life style.

If a central interest of this book is such macroscopic change, why study a small rural community? Jamaica's character, like that of many new states, is predominantly rural. Social scientists cannot ignore the impact of nationwide change on this segment of the population. Anthropologists have a particular contribution to make in the analyses of these processes. They have long been aware that the communities, villages, and tribes they studied were not isolated, self-contained social systems. The proliferation of new nation states and the dramatic changes that are occurring in developing countries throughout the world have led to a renewed interest in the manner in which nationwide changes affect rural communities. As Clifford Geertz has noted, "The method of anthropology—intensive, first-hand field study of small social units within the larger society—means that its primary contribution . . . lie[s] in a relatively microscopic and circumstantial analysis of a wide range of social processes as they appear in concrete form in this village, or that town, or the other social class."[3] Thus, the anthropologist is able to explore the way in which society-wide changes influence local culture and social structure, that is, beliefs, symbols, and values, on the one hand, and the existing network of social relations on the other.[4]

Although rural life in Jamaica has been studied by many anthropologists, these studies have generally ignored many formally structured institutions or have minimized the impact of the national system on the local community. For example, one set of anthropologists investigating rural Jamaican communities has chronicled those features of Jamaican rural life which can be considered evidence of a "folk" culture. Past work on rural Jamaicans has most frequently dealt with those aspects of their culture and social organization which differ most sharply from the dominant institutions and cultural traditions such as family life,[5] speech patterns,[6] folklore and music,[7] religious beliefs,[8] and economic life.[9]

* In 1891, 62.8 per cent of the classifiable labor force was engaged in agriculture, as opposed to 37.9 per cent in 1960.

The cumulative impression the outsider is likely to receive from reading the available studies of Jamaican rural communities is of a population living according to the quaint folk ways of its ancestors, in part an inheritance from African cultural traditions and the slavery experience, and in part a result of its isolation from the dominant institutions of the society.* Nothing could be further from the truth, and it would be difficult to overemphasize the extent to which rural Jamaicans are, and feel themselves to be, an integral part of an island-wide society. One of the underlying assumptions of this study is that Jamaican rural villagers are oriented to achieving goals which are structured by the national system of stratification: they desire prestigious and well-paid occupations and they want to live, as closely as possible, in the style of the island's elite. The opportunities available to realize these goals have, however, been very limited. Recent educational and political changes have, to some extent, improved the villagers' chances for realizing their status aspirations and have thus had an impact on life in rural communities. Just how they have affected one rural community is the subject of this study.[10]

* The blurb on the back cover of the recent edition of Martha Warren Beckwith's *Black Roadways: A Study of Jamaican Folk Life* is an extreme example of this trend: "Presented in this volume is a complete portrait of the black Jamaican peasantry, a people distinct in customs, religion, folklore, home life, and language from any other on earth, black or white . . . . In *Black Roadways* all aspects of the Jamaican peasant's rich and intriguing culture are examined, from his home life and his farming methods, to his childbirth rituals and his profound affinity with the supernatural."

PART I

The Setting

1

The Village of Coco Hill

Coco Hill is located in the north central Jamaican parish of St. Ann. Known as the "Garden Parish" because of its great beauty, St. Ann is a main center of both the bauxite and tourist industries. Kaiser Bauxite Company and Reynolds Jamaica Mines Ltd. operate mines and ports in St. Ann, have administrative offices there, and hold rights over thousands of acres of land, much of it still used for grazing cattle. Mining-related activities are responsible for the growth of a number of interior towns, Brown's Town and Claremont in particular, and for the improvement of the parish's roads. The tourist industry has grown rapidly over the past 15 years and is still growing. The north coast is dotted with big hotels and villas, and high-rise condominiums have been built in the principal tourist town, Ocho Rios. Traditionally, the parish has contained many large property holdings. Cattle and pimento (allspice) properties—many owned by Englishmen and Americans and managed by white Jamaicans—take up much of the land. There is a small but socially active planter set which focuses its activity around the St. Ann's Bay Polo Club, one of four such clubs on the island.

Coco Hill is a community of approximately 3,500 inhabitants, most of them poor, black farmers. I chose it for my study because it shares many characteristics with settlements formed by ex-slaves in inland,

mountainous Jamaica, and because it has been affected by such recent
developments as improved communications, increased government
services, development of local industries, and better markets for cash
crops.

The data upon which this study is based were collected between
July, 1968 and September, 1969, when I lived in the home of a Coco
Hill primary school teacher.* My data-gathering methods included in-
terviews, observation, and collection of biographical and genealogical
material. I also took a census of Percy Road, the section I lived in,
collecting such information as occupation, religious affiliation, land
ownership, place of birth, and household composition. I supplemented
my direct observations by consulting local police files, minutes of local
meetings, and government statistics on Coco Hill election results.
Finally, I examined published and unpublished historical studies and
documents.

At first there was some local suspicion about my activities—one
or two people believed me to be a spy, and several thought that I
represented the island tax board—but after a few weeks most of the
villagers accepted me as a fixture of community life. They became
used to seeing me on the roads and in the shops, welcomed my visits
to their homes, and helped me by giving whatever information they
could.

TYPES OF RURAL COMMUNITIES

According to the 1960 census, 65 per cent of Jamaica's population lives in strictly rural areas, 25 per cent in the two urban parishes
—Kingston and St. Andrew—and the rest in small towns.[1] While
every community is unique, it is useful to think of Jamaican rural communities in terms of five ideal types: small towns, sugar estates, settlements bordering sugar estates, remote hill communities, and more
prosperous villages populated largely by farmers. These types do not
represent an average, nor do they fully describe specific examples;
they do indicate the diversity of settlements and provide a "generalized rubric within which an indefinite number of particular cases may
be classified."[2] The typology helps to locate Coco Hill within the entire range of Jamaican rural communities.

The 22 towns of the island have traditionally been the foci of
agricultural activity. They are markets for produce grown in surrounding communities; a number serve as shipping ports for sugar, bananas,
and, in recent years, bauxite. The towns are, in addition, distribution

---

* The ethnographic present throughout the book is 1968–69.

centers for imported and manufactured goods; small supermarkets and stores which sell such products as clothing, furniture, and modern appliances are found there. The development of tourism and bauxite in the past 10 years has stimulated the growth of many rural towns; George Roberts notes that they have a much higher growth rate than strictly rural areas. In particular, stores and services catering to relatively well-paid bauxite employees and North American tourists have expanded. Numerous government services—for example, courts, hospitals, and agencies such as the Agricultural Marketing Corporation and Public Works Department—are located in these towns, as are doctors', dentists', and lawyers' offices. The population of the towns tends to be better educated and more highly skilled than that of more rural areas.

Sugar estates, the second type of settlement, are generally contiguous with town centers and most are located in the coastal areas of the island. As a result of the decline in the sugar industry, the number of this type of settlement is decreasing; in 1970 only 15 sugar estates with operating factories remained, one of them in the parish of St. Ann. Social life within these communities is affected by the requirements of the sugar industry—a large labor force is needed for about seven months of the year, while during the other five little work is available. There is thus an influx of labor into the community during crop season, and there are alternating periods of boom and depression, crop and dead season. Permanent residents on sugar estates form a nuclear labor force that can be relied on in times of emergency—for example, to put out a cane fire—and to perform necessary tasks such as planting during dead season. These workers usually cultivate ground plots, that is, small plots of land on which they grow subsistence, or ground, crops. Although some cultivate produce for sale at local markets, this is a secondary pursuit.

Settlements which border sugar estates represent the third type of community. Small farmers in these communities depend heavily upon estate work for cash, and usually cultivate their own small holdings in dead season, when there is not much demand for their labor on the estates. They produce crops for sale at internal markets as well as for their own use.

The fourth type of settlement consists of more remote hill communities whose poor, small farmers dispose of their surplus crops through the internal marketing system. The men often supplement their incomes by doing seasonal work at sugar estates. These settlements are geographically isolated, often reached only by unpaved roads, and lack electricity, water-supply systems, health clinics, and post offices. Few outsiders move into such communities, since they are not considered desirable places to live, and social relations within them are organized primarily around kinship and territorial ties. There are few associations and churches. Many who once lived in settlements of this type in the hills beyond Coco Hill—referred to as "up the mountain"—moved to more prosperous settlements because, as one man who had lived "up the mountain" told me, "Tear would come to your eye if you see the way them live up there."

More prosperous communities of small and medium farms compose the fifth type of settlement. Coco Hill belongs in this category. Members of these communities grow crops for their own use as well as for local and foreign markets, and they try to avoid working out at sugar estates. Their communities contain local school, post office, and health services, and have been provided with electricity, water-supply systems, and paved roads by the government. Farmers belong to branches of various national associations, and there are a number of churches. The growth of the bauxite, tourist, and smaller local industries, and the expansion of government services, have brought an influx of white-collar workers to these areas.

THE LOCAL SCENE

The villagers of Coco Hill live in several sections, on one of the four main roads or in the bush behind them. From the main roads one gets only a cursory glimpse of life in Coco Hill. Much of the cultivated land and many homesteads lie scattered in the interior, some off red dirt roads, others reached only by steep and often muddy trails winding through the bush.

Since so much of the land is used for farming, a description of agricultural practices in the community is helpful in understanding the life of the village. Land holdings fall into four categories: bought land, family land, inherited land, and rented land.[3] Bought land is property which has been purchased by the holder and can be used, transmitted, or disposed of according to his will. Similarly, inherited land can be sold by the holder. In contrast, family land is not supposed to be divided or sold except by consent of all of the holders, that is, the bilateral descendants of the original owner. Finally, rented land consists of plots of land for which individuals pay cash or percentages of yield.

In all sections of the community the custom is to plant "every little thing" throughout the year so that there is always something to sell at market. An overreliance on one or two crops is risky, since they may fetch a low price on the market or not come to fruition at all. It is not uncommon to see a square of land—an eighth of an acre—on which 12 or 15 crops are being grown.

The soil type and elevation of the various sections of Coco Hill are important in determining the crops that farmers grow. Cane Road —those sections of the community on the downhill road to the north coast—has St. Ann clay soil. This type of soil is fairly fertile and not very erodible. Cane Road has a warmer climate than other sections of Coco Hill since it is at a lower elevation. Bananas are a major crop in Cane Road and sugar cane is grown in quantity. There are also three pimento estates in this section which employ villagers in September and October to pick pimento. Ground provisions, that is, yams, sweet potatoes, and cocoes (root crops) are grown in Cane Road (and throughout Coco Hill) and form the staple diet throughout the community. In the other sections of Coco Hill the soil is more erodible and lower in nutrients, although it is easier to cultivate. In addition, their higher elevation means that winter night temperatures are often very low, and this stunts growth. Here farmers plant vegetables including carrots, corn, turnips, cabbages, and red peas. Citrus fruits, coffee, and bananas are also grown. Large estate owners in these sections use their land for grazing cattle.

As for methods of farming, farmers use a piece of land for four or five years and then leave it fallow. In this period they mulch—put branches of leaves and weeds in the fields to restore moisture to the soil—and manure the land. After about two years, they clear the piece, plow it, and start the cycle anew. The usual procedure is to leave one piece of land fallow at any given time; the size of that piece varies with the size of the farmer's holdings.

Cattle raising is undertaken on a large scale by a number of property owners, and on a smaller scale by successful farmers. The former raise cattle for slaughter, while small farmers sell milk locally, to the Bog Walk Condensary about 30 miles away, or to the hospital in St. Ann's Bay. Cows are an expensive investment—they cost about £50,* and require considerable land for grazing. Nearly everyone in Coco Hill has several fowl to provide eggs—and occasionally chicken —for the family, and a number also own pigs. Many farmers have donkeys which they use to ride to their fields and to carry loads.

The community itself is very picturesque. Its 1,300- to 2,000-foot elevation, varying from section to section, keeps summer temperatures comfortable, and the moderate climate is a source of pride to residents, who cannot understand how people in Kingston or along the coast manage to survive the lowland heat. From the top of the area's rolling

* At the time of this study, Jamaica was using sterling currency: £1 (one pound) = $2.40 (US); 1/ (one shilling) = 12¢ (US). This monetary standard and the above equivalents are those referred to throughout the book. Since this study was made, Jamaica has changed its monetary standard; the newly-created Jamaican dollar is worth about $1.25 (US).

green hills one can gaze down at the blue Caribbean. Despite these
attractions, only a few tourists venture into Coco Hill, although there
are an increasing number of rented cars and chauffeur-driven limou-
sines on the road, passing through on a new "mountain tour" which encourages visitors to see the "real Jamaica." To many Jamaicans, unaware
of or unimpressed by the community's increasing involvement with the
outside world, Coco Hill is still "bush."

COCO HILL AS A MEANINGFUL UNIT OF ANALYSIS

Persons in Coco Hill orient themselves to a number of social units
of varying territorial inclusiveness, depending on where they are at the
moment, to whom they are talking, and the situation which gives rise
to the discussion. To isolate any of these units—the household, the
neighborhood, the section, the community, the parish, or the nation—
for study is to create an artificial division, since social relations at each
level are interconnected. But individuals in Coco Hill do conceive of
their community as a bounded unit and as such it is a valid subject
for study.

It is, however, difficult to pinpoint exactly what and where Coco
Hill is. There are no absolute boundaries delimiting rural communities
in Jamaica, no village councils or other formal authority structures.
Individuals are mobile, going from one area to another to look for
work, visit kin, and attend market. Communities like Coco Hill consist
of scattered homesteads, and patchwork farms, which often take the
form of several small plots of land miles apart. Individuals are drawn
into contact with each other in shops, churches, schools, markets, health
clinics, nearby towns, and courts, but the boundaries of the areas that
these foci service vary, making it difficult to speak of a single community.

Nonetheless, in the minds of the inhabitants of Coco Hill, the
community is made up of discrete named sections on or off one of the
four roads. In response to the question, "What is Coco Hill?" I got a
wide variety of replies. Many people were anxious to pinpoint exact
boundary lines; some showed me a hill or rock which they believed to
mark a border. Others cited official divisions such as school districts or
postal zones. Some typical replies were:

When you say Coco Hill, mean the whole surrounding.

Coco Hill is like a country; Cane Road and Percy Road they
are the districts.

I was born on Percy Road, but I grew at Cane Road. But is
the same Coco Hill.

Only the center down there is Coco Hill and the post office
and all different sections come down to the post office.

People would explain that Coco Hill proper was really just the area
around the crossroads, where there are three rum shops, three grocery
stores, the police station, the betting shop, the People's Cooperative
Bank, the sanitation inspector's office, and two churches, and that the
outlying areas had their own names. However, there was general agreement about which sections constituted Coco Hill, and none of my
informants—who came from all sections—ever included certain areas
to the west or east as part of Coco Hill.

People consider the crossroads the capital of the village, and think
of the community as extending along the four roads. Individuals living
in each section, such as Cane Road, Kelly Road, and Percy Road, belong
to greater Coco Hill. Residents born in other communities are labeled
"strangers" in everyday conversation, though a person who was born
elsewhere but has lived in Coco Hill since childhood is generally not
considered a "stranger" and is recognized as a full-fledged member of
the community.

There is also strong loyalty to the parish of St. Ann. Although
individuals are mobile and many have lived in another parish at some
time,[4] there is generally a feeling of belonging to St. Ann and a greater
familiarity with communities and towns in St. Ann than with those in
other parishes.*

In many ways the section in which one lives is the most important
social unit. However, some social networks extend throughout Coco
Hill. The most important tie between individuals in different sections
is kinship. Indeed, many likened Coco Hill to one big family. They
explained that "we are all related," a fact genealogies confirmed. Even
"strangers" who did not move to the community specifically to join a
relative usually had relatives in Coco Hill. Kin are scattered throughout
the different sections; visiting is fairly frequent, and rituals such as
funerals and weddings bring together relatives from all parts of the
community. People would say, "Of course Cane Road and Percy Road
are part of Coco Hill. I have so many relatives there. We are all one."
This reflects an underlying feeling that it is one's relatives throughout
Coco Hill—often those with whom one grew up—who can be relied on
in times of need and to whom one feels emotionally close.

Unrelated individuals are brought into contact through schools,

* From a census of one section of Coco Hill, Percy Road: the majority, 86 per
cent of 184 adults, were born in the parish. Of those born in St. Ann, 37 per cent
were born on Percy Road, 26 per cent in one of the other sections of Coco Hill.
The remaining 37 per cent came from other parish communities, over 50 per cent
of these from communities within a 10-mile radius of Coco Hill.

churches, shops, and voluntary associations. Men meet each other on the way to their fields; they stop along the way to see friends as well as relatives, and say "how-de-do" to those they pass on the road. A number of men work together in local industries: three bakeries, a lime factory, and a block factory, and the larger estates draw workers from different sections. The men who work together often become friends. The associations cater to individuals from every section and the leaders from the entire area form informal cliques. Although women tend to be more sedentary than men, spending more time in their own neighborhoods and traveling to the fields less, they do stand on the road and talk to passersby, frequent the shops, and go to the post office, churches, and nearby market towns.

There is also a great deal of intersectional mobility; 20 per cent of the adults on Percy Road, for example, had moved there from another section of the community in the past 10 years. The ties to ex-neighbors as such seemed to be minimal, unless kept alive by other bonds such as kinship, church membership, farming adjacent plots of land, and, among the white-collar workers, big farmers, and entrepreneurs, common status aspirations. Residential mobility within the community brings a wide range of people—both kin and non-kin—into an individual's universe, and broadens his view of what Coco Hill is.

COCO HILL AS A CHANGING COMMUNITY

Coco Hill's history is unwritten. The memories of present-day inhabitants are not only tinged with nostalgia but are biased by each informant's social position and past experience. An interesting example of how people view the past and the difficulties of getting the facts are highlighted by an account given me by a former Parish Councillor for the area, a man of about 90, the son of a big landowner, a Justice of the Peace, and one of the most respected citizens of Coco Hill. He is a fair-skinned man of German and Scotch descent and still vividly recalls the days when Coco Hill was dominated by large properties. According to him, "Slavery was abolished through the Baptists and they approached Queen Victoria and she paid out the landowners in Jamaica. They did farming, plant bananas and coconuts, they get a big income. Is the same slave people that was dismissed did come to settle in this area. Not like now, a better class. No black power business, they respected the white people."

From what I could gather, during slave-holding days property in Coco Hill was owned by absentee Englishmen and run by white managers and overseers. Most of the land was divided into citrus, coconut, coffee, or pimento estates; some of the land was used by the slaves to plant ground provisions, which they both used and sold. After the abolition of slavery many slaves bought small holdings from their former owners. Others merely squatted on unoccupied land, significant numbers coming up from the coastal sugar areas to settle. Many of the sections of Coco Hill got their names from the original landowners; for example, Mitchell Road is named after a Mr. Mitchell and Coco Hill was originally named Edwards Town, after an English proprietor.

Many of the large properties in the area have long since been sold and subdivided, owned and used by Coco Hill residents for over a century. In the past 20 years, two properties of over 1,000 acres each have been subdivided and sold. However, Coco Hill is still hemmed in on each side by properties of over 500 acres. One is owned by a black family from another parish who bought the land from the English owners in the late nineteenth century. Four are owned by white Jamaicans and one is owned by a very fair-skinned Jamaican.

Changes other than those of land distribution have affected the community in recent decades. In 1945, Coco Hill was a "bush" area with no paved roads, no electricity, no post office, no police station, no public school building and a population engaged almost exclusively in agriculture. In the space of two decades it has, in the eyes of many inhabitants, almost qualified for the designation of a town.

This is not to say that Coco Hill was ever an isolated or entirely self-contained community. Individuals in rural Jamaican communities have always been drawn into the central institutions of the society through schools, churches, courts, and the presence of representatives of the island's elite—white planters, ministers, government officials, and teachers. Farmers were never merely subsistence cultivators but produced crops for local and foreign markets.* Individuals have always been fairly mobile, moving in search of work, traveling to and from market, visiting kin in different towns and parishes, and using services available in larger towns. There has also been, since the end of the nineteenth century, considerable out-migration to Kingston, other parishes, and "foreign parts" in search of wage employment.

However, in the past 10 to 25 years, Coco Hill has become more closely integrated into the mainstream of Jamaican society. In the first place, the population has both changed in character and expanded.

---

* The development of export crops among the ex-slaves may be traced to the decline in sugar prices in the 1840's. There were fewer opportunities for wage employment on the sugar estates and the settlers had to turn to their holdings for cash. The decline in estate production also meant a decline in the demand for staple foodstuffs. Settlers were therefore driven to produce export crops in order to provide themselves with cash incomes to buy imported food, clothing, and other consumer goods. Gisela Eisner, *Jamaica 1830–1930: A Study in Economic Growth* (Manchester: Manchester University Press, 1961), pp. 210–235.

The local population growth stems not only from a decreasing infant mortality rate (and general death rate), but from an influx of people to the area. One bauxite company bought up a large property in the community and settled about 300 farmers, displaced by mining operations elsewhere in the parish, on it. The growth of government services has meant that more government workers—teachers, agricultural officers, prison wardens, nurses, policemen, public health workers, and probation officers—have come to Coco Hill. The development of industry in areas around Coco Hill has drawn in a number of white-collar residents who work in nearby towns. For example, as rents continue to rise in areas closer to the mines and offices, it is becoming more common for employees of the St. Ann bauxite companies to rent homes in Coco Hill.

There has also been some industrial development within the community. Coco Hill's lime factory was built in the early 1940's to process the limestone which is mined nearby. It provides employment for unskilled manual workers; although it now employs only 44 men (about half from neighboring communities), before the installation of electricity, over 90 men worked there. In the late 1950's a block factory was built. It employs about 15 men and supplies building materials for the community and adjacent areas. Two of the three bakeries have been built in the past 30 years; one dates from the early 1940's, the other from the early 1960's. Together they employ over 30 men.

The expansion of government agricultural schemes and programs, such as the 1962–67 Five Year Programme, has meant that farmers in Coco Hill are more directly affected by government policies than they were before independence. For example, the sale of bananas, a major crop in the community, always sensitive to world market conditions and preferential trade agreements with Britain, is now controlled by the government's Banana Board. The price which the grower receives is determined by the subsidy which the government decides to pay; this in turn is determined by the price the United Kingdom sets and the quantity of fruit it buys, as well as competition from other West Indian producers. The sale of produce to local markets also depends on government subsidies. For example, the subsidy on pig feed in 1967 encouraged many farmers to raise pigs. There are now so many on the market, and the price for them is so low, that people complain it costs them more to keep the animals alive than they can ever hope to make by selling them—a situation which was aggravated when the government, in an attempt to alleviate the problem, eliminated the subsidy on pig feed.

Not everyone stays in Coco Hill. There has been migration to other countries since the end of the nineteenth century, but the destination of the migrants has changed. In the past, rural Jamaicans went to Cuba to work on the sugar estates and to Central America to work on banana plantations or aid in building railways and the Panama Canal. During World War II, a number of men traveled to the United States on farm contract schemes, stayed for about a year, and returned home. About 30 men still work "on the contract" in the United States, spending part of the year cultivating their land in Coco Hill and part on farms in America. In the late 1950's and early 1960's, before Great Britain placed strict limitations on West Indian immigration, many Jamaicans went to England in search of work. Today, people in Coco Hill have set their sights on going to the United States and Canada to find nonagricultural jobs in the big cities. Because there is a demand for domestic labor in North American cities, it is much easier for women than men to get visas and jobs. Nearly every week one hears of another woman from Coco Hill who has left for the United States—usually New York City— or Canada. In fact, many saw me as a messiah who had come to provide a way for them to get to the United States. I was besieged by requests to get people sponsors and jobs in the United States, and still get letters with similar pleas.

Nearly everyone in Coco Hill has a close relative in either the United States or England and receives letters and parcels from them. Relatives also send money to those who have remained behind; the Post Mistress of Coco Hill estimates that villagers receive about £200 a week in postal orders. A number of parents have been able to send their children to secondary school with funds sent back from abroad; many send their children overseas to join prospering relatives. Several houses in Coco Hill are being built by people who were "in foreign." This evidence of success and tales of affluence on foreign shores have aroused in nearly all a desire to "travel," to work for a few years, and accumulate enough money to return home to live in comparative comfort.

When asked what things were like in Coco Hill in the old days, many residents referred to the fact that because there were fewer people there were fewer houses, and that those few were not as nice as those going up today. Formerly, many houses were built by a method known as nogging: a wooden frame was strengthened with stones, lime, and red earth, and roofed with wooden shingles. Others were merely wattle and daub structures. With loans increasingly available to small farmers, greater aspirations resulting from improved education and communications, and welfare programs sponsored by the central government, houses built since the 1940's have been made of concrete blocks and marl, with zinc roofs.

A major village problem has been, and still is, the water-supply system. Only one section of Coco Hill has piped water and even this is a recent development. In "bygone" days people fetched water from the springs and rivers running through the community. Since the 1950's, the government has built two public catchment tanks, and many residents have built their own.

Postal facilities have greatly improved over the years. Some of the oldest inhabitants remember when a courier would go to the post office in a nearby town to mail the letters he had collected in Coco Hill and to pick up letters and parcels. A postal agency * was brought to Coco Hill at the turn of the century, housed at first in a small shop and moved to its own government-rented building in 1952 when it became a post office. Mail continued to be carried on foot and by bicycle until 1954, when the red Royal Mail vans came on the scene and replaced the courier. Cane Road acquired a separate postal agency in the early 1960's, which eliminated the need for people in that section to travel to Coco Hill for mail, although they still must go there to send telegrams and to receive and send packages.

Prior to 1954, there was no school building in Coco Hill; classes were held in various churches. The local teaching staff increased from five in 1943 to 17 in 1968, and an infant school for children under six has also been built.

Until 1943 there were no policemen in the area and district constables maintained the peace. In the late 1940's regular police patrols were sent to the community from St. Ann's Bay, the parish capital, and in 1948 a two-man police post was established. At first the police station was located in the house of a prosperous farmer, but in 1955 the station moved to its own building at the crossroads. In 1968 it took over a modern building in the same area.

Electricity came to some parts of Coco Hill in 1949, enabling more fortunate residents to purchase radios, refrigerators, television sets, and other modern appliances, as well as to use electric light. Cane Road did not get electricity until 1967, and many areas in the bush off the main roads still do not have it. Even where installation is possible, many families are too poor to use "current" and must rely on traditional kerosene lamps.

Over half the households in Coco Hill have radios, and a few even possess television sets. Those without electricity have battery-run radios and can tune in the two Jamaican radio stations. It is amazing to walk through a bush area along a winding dirt path and hear soul tunes and "reggae" (a Jamaican dance) blasting forth from every house. The latest pop tunes are played at full volume over sound

---

* A post office differs from a postal agency in Jamaica in that one cannot receive or send telegrams or parcels at a postal agency.

systems installed in the rum shops; the young folk are never far behind the Kingston crowd in knowing the latest songs and dances. News programs and information broadcasts as well as soap operas and religious programs—Jamaican, English, and American—are broadcast by both radio stations. One woman explained that she wrote to a cousin in America every week to keep her up-to-date on the latest happenings in "Dulcimena: Her Life in Town," a local soap opera which chronicles the trials and tribulations of a poor black country girl who has migrated to Kingston. With their radios, people in Coco Hill can follow events in the world at large. A number of men stayed up all night listening to the 1968 American presidential election returns, and many closely followed the details of the moon landing.

Newspapers are another source of information about the world outside Coco Hill. Before World War II, the only way to get a newspaper was to have it sent by post, and it arrived a day late. Since the late 1940's, *The Daily Gleaner,* Jamaica's only morning paper, has been distributed throughout the area and reaches Coco Hill by 10:00 a.m. Approximately 85 people receive the paper from its local distributor. They either come for the paper in person or buy it from one of the several vendors who peddle it in the community.

In 1930 there was only one shop—owned by a Chinese man—in Coco Hill; today there are 28 grocery shops along the four roads, one dry goods store, and one supermarket.* Although the Parish Councillor promised that a phone booth would soon be installed and although work has begun on telephone lines, Coco Hill still does not have a public telephone. Prior to 1962 those who wanted to see a doctor had to go to one of the nearby towns or visit one of the several doctors who made weekly visits to Coco Hill and held clinic in someone's home. Although most people still do this and pay regular fees, since 1962 there has been a health clinic in the community, visited weekly by a doctor who charges only 2/- a visit. A district nurse also makes daily visits to see to minor complaints and a dentist visits the clinic once a week.

The prison, established in 1949, occupies an area formerly known as the common, an area where people picnicked and played cricket. It employs 23 warders, most of them native to Coco Hill and all living in the community. High atop a hill, the prison is almost completely

---

* The supermarket in Coco Hill is merely a large shop. Unlike other shops in the community it offers a wide assortment of imported goods, and, having a refrigerator, sells milk, ice cream, and butter. Its classification as a supermarket derives from the fact that a customer can wander down the three aisles, select the items he wishes to buy, and bring them to the shopowner at the cash register. In the other shops, the shopkeeper stands behind the counter and hands over the goods the customer wishes to purchase.

separate from the community, and although uniformed warders are a frequent sight on the roads, the prisoners are seen only on Sundays, when they are marched out in white uniforms to attend the various churches.

Transportation has also improved over the years. The elderly Post Mistress fondly remembers when she and her family would pile into a horse-drawn buggy to ride to church on Sunday. Poorer folk, however, bitterly recall the days when they had to walk nine miles to market, carrying goods on their heads or on donkeys. Twenty years ago no buses came through the area and there were only three cars and four trucks in all Coco Hill. A person who wanted to go to Kingston had to travel by horse and cart for about 15 miles to reach a point where public transport was available. Roads were not asphalted until the early 1950's; there was no paved road to the north coast until the early 1960's and it was only in 1968 that the road to a market town in the hills was completed. The bus to Kingston began to run in 1948 and bus routes to nearby towns were added with the years. Today there is a daily bus to and from St. Ann's Bay, Kingston, and Montego Bay. A number of people run private van (small bus) services to market towns on Wednesday and Saturday. One local resident runs a bus service and three vans to various parts of the parish, another runs a van service to transport children to and from secondary schools in nearby towns. Many people own cars and trucks—there are over 35 private motor vehicles in Coco Hill, some used part of the time as taxis.

Improvements in transportation have increased physical mobility. Coco Hill's white-collar residents have acquaintances throughout a large area, and are on intimate terms with those of similar status who live long distances away. Young men under 25 tend to regard Coco Hill as a home base from which to make frequent trips to Kingston and other towns in search of work, and have friends in these places. It is also much easier for people today to visit kin in other communities; all have kin in other parts of Jamaica, and nearly all have at least one relative in Kingston. I found very few people in Coco Hill who had not been to Kingston at least once in the past year, and people go to one of the nearby market towns at least once a month.

As Coco Hill has been drawn into relations with the outside world, it has been the scene of what is known as a revolution of rising expectations. Improved communications, reports from those who have migrated, the increasing scope of the government's educational, agricultural, and social welfare programs, and the growth of tourism, industry, and commerce have, in the words of a Jamaican sociologist, made it possible "for some to achieve their expectations and raised the hopes of doing so in thousands more." [5]

Although changes in the past two decades have brought the residents of Coco Hill into closer contact with the dominant institutions of Jamaican society, the impact of these changes is filtered through the local system of status differentiation. It is this crucial dimension of the local social system to which we now turn.

II

The Local Status System

Like other rural Jamaican communities, Coco Hill appears at first to be relatively undifferentiated. The community's poor, black farmers rank at the bottom of the island-wide class/status hierarchy. Yet within Coco Hill status distinctions do exist and are important in structuring the villagers' behavior and attitudes. In discussing the local system of status differentiation, I shall show how status * is perceived by the residents, how it can be defined in terms of selected objective criteria, and the relationship between the local system of prestige ranking and the island-wide stratification system.

RANKING BY COMMUNITY MEMBERS

Just how do the villagers view the local status structure? What criteria do they use for determining status in their community? In seeking answers to these questions I asked the 101 household heads on Percy Road who they considered the most respected people in Coco Hill, and why. The 41 names they listed fell into a number of categories;

* I shall use Weber's definition of status, that is "every typical component in the life fate of men that is determined by a specific, positive or negative, social estimation of honor." H. Gerth and C. Wright Mills, eds., *From Max Weber: Essays in Sociology,* Galaxy Books (New York: Oxford University Press, 1958), p. 187.

many of the criteria they used are the same ones social scientists employ to uncover the objective dimensions of a status system.

In explaining why they named certain individuals, those interviewed emphasized income, financial position, life style, and occupation. "They have their own income . . . they can build a nice home and can afford to buy things for your comfort . . . all those employ the poorer classes . . . up class people them." Many stressed the independence gained from income and occupation. "People who don't have to work out . . . live independent, don't have to live off anybody." Others described the behavior which they associated with respectability. "They conduct themselves well . . . they are true Christians . . . they don't drink or gossip on the road . . . they live up to principles . . . they act a decent way, them true-hearted people, move correct." Finally, a number mentioned the relations that respected people had with their neighbors in Coco Hill. "Are decent and kind to people . . . you can approach them for help . . . you can depend on them."

A numerical breakdown of the answers reveals that 61 persons mentioned qualities that referred to the individual's social status while 52 mentioned behavioral or moral qualities. Of these latter, only four specifically stated that poor people * could be respectable; no poor people were listed in answer to the first question. The others indicated, either by specific comments or by the persons they named, that "acting decent" was only one reason for their choice, since those named had relatively high occupational and economic status in the community. Certain kinds of behavior are expected of those in high status positions in Coco Hill. For example, helping others is a status-related trait mentioned by 10 residents of Percy Road; such help consists of loans, gifts, old clothes, rides, and other favors which only relatively well-off villagers can afford to give.

"Living independent" is a popular phrase in Coco Hill, and 12 respondents noted the independence associated with assured incomes and prestigious occupations. To the villagers, independence means that one does not need to work out in menial capacities or ask others for loans and favors but can, instead, hire labor and dispense favors. In this sense many white-collar workers are considered independent, although they depend on the government and private companies for their salaries.

BASES OF STRATIFICATION

Many residents of Coco Hill perceive that financial position is the most crucial factor in determining status in the community. This is pri-

* By poor people, I mean wage laborers.

marily because income determines life style. In turn, income depends
on occupation and/or the amount of land owned. The other variables
involved in status differentiation—leadership, residence, color, education, age, and sex—are bases for prestige only in combination with
these other factors.

Five broad status groups,* characterized by occupation, land
ownership, income, and life style may be distinguished: ** wage
laborers, small independent farmers, big farmers and entrepreneurs,
white-collar workers, and large estate owners. Wage laborers are those
who own less than three acres of land, and in some cases, no land at all,
and supplement their incomes by working for others. They are never
in a position to hire labor, and when they work out it is generally in
such menial jobs as work for small farmers, in the case of men, and
domestic work, in the case of women. Small independent farmers own
between three and 10 acres of land, sometimes less if they have an
additional occupation. Such occupations include working out in a
trade—for example, carpentry or tailoring—or at one of the small local
factories, in the case of men, and sewing and higglering,*** in the case
of women. They rarely work out for others in menial capacities, and
hire the labor of others at infrequent intervals. Big farmers are those
who own between 10 and 50 acres of land. They never work in menial
capacities for others, although they may follow an additional occupation—shopkeeping, for example—and they employ wage labor
regularly. Often their wives are higglers. Successful shopkeepers, truck
owners, van operators, and bakery owners are classified as entrepreneurs. White-collar workers do not engage in agricultural activities.
They are salaried employees who work in offices in nearby towns, often
in nonmanual posts with the bauxite companies. Government civil
servants—teachers, post office clerks, agricultural officers, nurses, and
probation officers—are also included in this category. Large estate
owners are those with more than 100 acres of land. They regularly hire
large numbers of wage laborers.

* I use the term "status group" to refer to people who share certain social
characteristics, but may not be aware of their common location in the social
structure or constitute an interacting social group.

** On the basis of a census of Percy Road, estimates by knowledgeable
villagers, and my own estimates of the rest of the village, the proportion of the
population in each category is: wage laborers, 36 per cent; small farmers, 45 per
cent; big farmers and entrepreneurs, 10 per cent; white-collar workers, eight per
cent; and large estate owners, one per cent.

*** A higgler is a woman who buys and sells produce. Higglers in the village
usually buy fruits and vegetables from farmers in Coco Hill and sell them in
Kingston or nearby towns. In addition, some buy products at market to sell in
Coco Hill. For a fuller discussion of higglers in Jamaica, see Katzin, op. cit.

Occupation and Land Ownership

It is apparent that occupation and land ownership are the most important factors in determining status in Coco Hill.* Occupation and land ownership not only enable individuals to maintain certain life styles, but structure the kinds of social relations a person has with others in the community. This, in turn, affects his prestige. When wage laborers interact with those who are not wage laborers it is generally in a subordinate role. The fact that they own little or no land and do not possess the skills to pursue other occupations means that they are forced to engage in low status and menial occupations to meet their cash needs. They take on a subordinate role, not only in the work situation, but in other social situations. For example, they must often buy water from neighbors who own catchment tanks, beg rides from white-collar workers, get credit at shops, and ask for old clothes and other favors from better-off villagers. Many wage laborers, as well as a number of less successful small farmers, depend on higglers to sell their crops. Women who do higglering tend to be the wives of more prosperous small farmers, big farmers, and entrepreneurs. They are often accused of cheating villagers and lying to them about market prices. At the same time, many higglers complain that they suffer from fluctuations in market prices and that they frequently lose money because they have promised a fixed rate for the crops they buy from villagers, a rate which they do not always receive at market. However, a profit is usually made in such arrangements, and women would not continue to do higglering if this were not the case. Since 1963, farmers who cannot afford the time or money to go to market or who prefer to avoid personal entanglements with higglers have been able to sell their produce to the Agricultural Marketing Corporation. This government organization has a branch in a nearby town and sends a truck to collect produce from farmers in Coco Hill at regular intervals. Using the services of the Agricultural Marketing Corporation saves time and assures the farmer that all of his produce will be bought. However, many wage laborers and small farmers continue to rely on higglers, who can often get a better price for their crops.

* Most villagers do not follow one occupation but, in the phrase coined by Lambros Comitas, are "occupational pluralists." See Comitas, *op. cit.* A man may cultivate a few acres of land but he may also practice a trade, go to the United States to work on the farm contract scheme, work on the road when such employment is available, or sell his labor to other farmers in the district. On Percy Road, 33 per cent of all adult males farmed on a full-time basis, 40 per cent farmed and followed an additional occupation, and 27 per cent did no farming at all. For details of the occupational distribution of the adults on Percy Road see Appendix.

Small independent farmers rarely hire labor and seldom work out for other villagers in a menial role. In fact, those who pursue other occupations, such as tradesman or seamstress, enjoy contact with others in a role which enhances their prestige, since a tradesman or seamstress is respected for his or her skill. Although small farmers stress that they try to "live independent," they are, in fact, dependent on those in higher status positions. For example, they usually credit their goods at local shops, and ask for favors such as car rides and loans from those in still better positions.

Individuals in other status groups, as employers of labor, come into contact with many villagers in a superordinate role. Most big farmers have two or three regular field hands and during busy seasons may hire up to 10 or 12 men. Successful entrepreneurs regularly employ labor, control credit, and serve as middlemen in the transportation and sale of cash crops. For example, growers of sugar and bananas must pay the local truckmen to carry their produce to the sugar factory, five miles away, and to the banana-boxing plant, 10 miles away. White-collar workers regularly employ men and boys to care for their yards, and women to clean their homes and care for their children. In addition, teachers, nurses, agricultural officers, and other government civil servants interact with villagers from positions which are endowed with the legitimacy and prestige of the government. They are also local experts on such matters as education and agricultural policies and are often sought out for information on these topics as well as for general favors. Finally, estate owners maintain a staff of household help and regularly employ many agricultural workers. Besides giving rides to villagers, they are frequently approached for relatively large loans.

Further analysis reveals that among those persons respected by Percy Road residents, the majority, 86 per cent, belonged to the top three status groups. Only 14 per cent were small independent farmers; no wage laborers were mentioned. Of those mentioned most frequently, that is, by more than five persons, two were estate owners, seven were big farmers or entrepreneurs, and five were white-collar workers. They not only maintain a respectable life style, but play a superordinate role in their frequent contact with large numbers of the population.

Life Style

The type of house a person lives in, the clothes he wears, the people with whom he associates on an equal basis, and the number of modern appliances he can buy are just a few of the symbols of prestige in Coco Hill. While none of the villagers has an income which enables him to buy the new gadgets advertised on radio and in the newspaper, or to live in homes comparable to those of the Kingston middle class, there is intense competition focused around consumption ability. Such competition rarely occurs between members of different status groups, but among persons who are very close in the local status hierarchy. As Thorstein Veblen has noted in *The Theory of the Leisure Class*, "In any community where goods are held in severalty it is necessary, in order to his [sic] own peace of mind, that an individual should possess as large a portion of goods as others with whom he is accustomed to class himself; and it is extremely gratifying to possess something more than others." [1]

Wage laborers, at the bottom of the local status hierarchy, can least afford to consume conspicuously, although they do attempt to purchase items which symbolize prestige and to compete with one another in such purchasing. Often a wage laborer, living in a poor shack in the bush, will own a new table and chair set bought recently on credit from the local dry goods store. However, in general, wage laborers cannot afford, as they express it, to "live the life"; they live in run-down shacks, usually having only one room, without electricity or other modern conveniences. Since Coco Hill does not have a piped water system, the residents must either use the public tank (and most do not like to do this since the public tank is not well enclosed, animals frequently have access to it, and dung is often found floating in the water), catch water in big oil drums, or build private catchment tanks, an enterprise which costs at least £150. The way in which one gets water has become a measure of prestige in the community, especially since those who own private tanks often sell water to their less fortunate neighbors, the going rate being a penny a potful. "Tankless" villagers must approach those who own tanks in a subordinate and low status role. Wage laborers can usually afford only one or two big drums and therefore often depend on neighbors or the public tank for water. Coco Hill is a very wet area; rarely does a week pass without at least one heavy downpour, even in the dry season from July to August. Nonetheless, one or two drums do not provide sufficient water for a family's cooking and washing needs.

Independent small farmers have an income which enables them to live in larger dwellings, usually two- and three-room houses with electricity. They have few modern appliances, sometimes only a radio, and six or seven drums to catch water. In times of drought they too must go to more prosperous neighbors to purchase water. The women in such households often have sewing machines and make most of the clothes for their households. Much effort and expense is lavished on furnishing the homes and in keeping them neat and tidy; many women wash and polish their floors once a day. In these homes, it is not uncommon for visitors to take off their shoes when they enter, in recognition of their hostesses' meticulous housekeeping; few follow this practice when entering a wage laborer's dwelling. These independent farming families proudly display their wedding gifts—dishes, glassware, and serving pieces—in glass-fronted wooden cabinets; pictures of successful relatives, often sent from abroad, are pasted on the cabinets, next to pictures of the Queen, Jamaican political leaders, Jesus Christ, and even John F. Kennedy or Martin Luther King. Women in these households take great pride in the clothes they wear to church and to special events such as funerals or weddings. While a family may not eat beef for weeks, the woman of the household will make a new dress for every wedding or funeral she attends. Although she does the sewing herself, expensive material—costing as much as £1 a yard—is often used. A relatively large amount of money is also spent on household decorations and furnishings. For example, one woman had three bedspreads of different colors which she changed periodically; she had only one very old and soiled sheet to use underneath.

Big farmers and entrepreneurs live in still larger and better-furnished dwellings and generally own such modern appliances as a refrigerator. All have catchment tanks. While most women in this group make their own clothes, some of the more prosperous own a number of store-bought dresses, which they reserve for church meetings and other special occasions. One of the symbols of big farmers' status is the number of cows they own. Prosperous big farmers may own as many as 10 or 15 cows and have special water tanks for them on their grazing land.

White-collar workers in Coco Hill tend to be "strangers" who have only recently risen to white-collar status. The majority come from prosperous farming families in other parts of the island and have qualified for their relatively prestigious and well-paid occupations by attending secondary school or training college, or by passing examinations. While most white-collar workers are aware that they are part of the island's lower-middle class, they are most anxious to dissociate themselves from farmers in Coco Hill and to identify, as closely as possible, with the middle classes in Kingston and bigger country towns. This is done largely through consumption, although education and cultural characteristics associated with education, such as speech patterns and manners, also play a role in validating their status. Because they have relatively large and steady incomes, they are able to outdo other villagers in consuming conspicuously. They have modern furniture in their homes and many modern appliances such as televisions and refrigerators. Unlike villagers in the other groups, who cook over wood fires in separate kitchen shacks in back of their homes, white-collar workers have indoor kitchens with kerosene or gas stoves. They also have indoor toilets, and regard the pit latrines used by others in the community as common. Inside, their homes are decorated with crochet work, artificial flowers, and so on. (A teacher who had recently built a new home in Coco Hill was deeply offended when another teacher, after viewing the house for the first time, spread the rumor that there was no crochet work on display.) Several sets of curtains and bedspreads are rotated regularly. High school and university pictures of successful relatives are displayed. Clothes are usually store-bought and of the latest style; unlike women in other groups, white-collar women straighten their hair and they never appear in what they regard as the cheap and ordinary styles which farming women wear. Many of the white-collar workers own automobiles, although it is only the man in the family who knows how to drive; cars, as well as being evidence of success and achievement, allow them to maintain friendships with individuals of similar status in other villages and parishes. While farming villagers ride atop donkeys or walk to work in their fields, white-collar workers use their cars to go distances as short as a quarter of a mile.

Coco Hill's few estate owners are secure in their position vis-a-vis the villagers, and compete for status with fellow estate owners, who reside in other villages and parishes. Their large old houses, situated atop high hills overlooking the estates, are furnished not with imported North American furniture or local copies of it, but with antiques and heirlooms which emphasize their connection with established planting families.

Leadership

Another correlate of status in the village, closely linked to occupation and land ownership, is official position in one of the local branches of six national associations—the Jamaica Agricultural Society, All-Island Banana Growers' Association, People's Cooperative Bank, Parent Teachers Association, Credit Union, Coffee Growers' Cooperative *— or one of the local churches—Anglican, Methodist, Baptist, Roman Catholic, Tabernacle Baptist, Seventh Day Adventist, Church of God, and Pentecostal.

Leaders in the village associations tend to be big farmers, entrepreneurs, or white-collar workers. While these associations are

---

* See Chapter VIII for a discussion of the status-conferring functions of position in the local branches of the national political parties.

relatively ineffective in influencing outside agencies and attendance at the meetings is generally low, most community residents know who the leaders are, and an official position enhances a person's prestige. A post in certain of the groups also provides some influence locally. For example, the officials of the bank and the credit union decide who receives loans, and officials of the Coffee Growers' Cooperative collect coffee from farmers, arrange for it to be shipped to the processing plant, and distribute the dividends which are handed down from the national office.

Similarly, a great deal of prestige accrues from the role of elder or deacon in the local churches. Coco Hill residents are avid churchgoers. Many attend services once or twice a week, and the church has profound moral authority in their eyes. Only two of the local churches have a resident minister. Local elders officiate at most church services; the official ministers of the other churches come to Coco Hill once or twice a month. The deacons and elders—the term varies according to the church—preach, supervise Sunday school classes and the financial affairs of the church, serve on informal courts which try members for committing "sinful" offenses, and are often sought out for advice by the brethren. Their positions not only give them a superordinate role in relation to many of their neighbors, but endow them with the charisma of the church. These leaders are often the same men who are active in the associations, but in four churches—Baptist Tabernacle, Church of God, Seventh Day Adventist, and the Pentecostal Church—some of the elders are small farmers. While not all those considered respected were even members of the voluntary associations, about half were either officials or church elders.

The most prestigious political office in the community is the formal position of Justice of the Peace, which has traditionally been associated with white estate owners. Justices of the Peace are appointed by the Custos * of the parish upon recommendation by local associations or, more often, political parties. They sit in judgment at Petty Sessions Courts, have the power to validate documents such as land transfers, bail bonds, and bank papers and, at certain social events, mingle with people important in parish affairs. In recent years more black men— professionals, merchants, and relatively large farmers—have been appointed. In Coco Hill, three Justices of the Peace are of the traditional type: they are all estate owners; two are fair-skinned and one is white. The most recently appointed Justice of the Peace, however, is a

---

* The Custos is the chief magistrate of the parish and is appointed by the Governor-General upon the recommendation of the Prime Minister. His principal responsibility is to make recommendations to the Ministry of Home Affairs concerning the appointment of Justices of the Peace in the parish.

black man who was recommended for the position by the local branch of the People's National Party. He owns about 45 acres of land, heads the People's Cooperative Bank, and is an official in many local associations. His position as Justice of the Peace greatly enhances his prestige: he is continually asked to sign documents ("Yesterday when I was in the field, 11 came to me"); he sits in judgment in the courts; and he is able to expand his circle of political and social acquaintances in the parish. This man was listed as a respected person by 18 respondents, making him second in status only to the fair-skinned Justice of the Peace.

Color and Education

There is a definite bias in favor of whites in Coco Hill. Many black wage laborers associate their poverty with color and nearly all have an unquestioning acceptance of the superiority and beauty of white skin. This is not hard to understand, since until very recently there was a close correlation between class and color in Jamaican society, with whites and coloreds at the top of the hierarchy and blacks at the bottom. While many blacks have moved into prestigious positions (during the late 1960's, the Prime Minister and the Governor-General were very dark-skinned men), the lower class in Jamaica is predominantly black. However, within Coco Hill color is not in itself the basis for social groupings, and is a basis for prestige only in combination with income, occupation, land ownership, and life style. Having light skin does not automatically entitle a person to deference. Many fair-skinned persons are anxious to dissociate themselves from blacks, and try to claim prestige on the basis of their color. These claims are regarded as illegitimate by fellow villagers, who think of their neighbors as black because they dress and live in a manner associated with poor Jamaican blacks. Nearly 75 per cent of those listed as respected were black or very dark skinned.

While everyone in Coco Hill is sensitive to the slightest gradations of skin color—as well as to other racial attributes such as "good" hair, straight nose, and thin lips—it is the dark-skinned white-collar workers who are most concerned with the status-conferring functions of light skin. On the one hand, they have an unquestioning acceptance of the superiority of white skin, illustrated by one teacher's comment that there were no ugly whites. They would like their children to "marry up" in color terms, that is, to marry a lighter-skinned person. When they describe someone, skin color is inevitably mentioned. On the other hand, they adamantly deny that color plays a role in status placement. Instead, they assert that there are more important manifestations of status—dress and speech patterns, for example—by which they distinguish themselves from the poor farmers in Coco Hill. They emphasize that the "common" people have no manners, often saying that the latter do not use knives or forks. White-collar workers wear fashionable clothes when they leave their homes, straighten their hair (if they are women), and speak "proper" English, instead of the patois spoken by the villagers. More important, they claim that it is ability and education above all else which merit deference, stressing their superior achievements as justification for their own claims to prestige. Those who have attended a training college or high school—as most of this group have—maintain their school ties and friendships with "batchmates," that is, individuals in the same graduating class.

With the exception of the white-collar workers and estate owners, who together make up about nine per cent of the adult population of the community, educational attainment is not a factor in the local system of status differentiation. Most adults in Coco Hill have not gone beyond the sixth grade of primary school; the majority attended irregularly. No farmers or entrepreneurs had passed the Jamaica Local Examinations given at the primary school to qualify school-leavers for such occupations as teaching; those who passed the exams did not remain in farming or small-scale business. However, as we shall see in later chapters, their children's educational attainments are a source of prestige for adults in the community. Of those mentioned as respected, nearly all had one child or more who had passed the Jamaica Local Examinations or attended training college or secondary school.

Residence, Age, and Sex

Residential location is not a significant factor in status differentiation in Coco Hill, although there are some distinctions in the community, primarily between living "on the main" or "in the bush." Those on the main roads are nearer to shops and transportation, and generally have electricity, whereas those who live off rocky dirt paths in the bush are often as far as two miles from a main road and do not have electric lines in their area. There is also a distinction between Cane Road, comprising the lower sections of the community, on the road to the north coast, and Coco Hill, comprising the upper sections. Residents of Cane Road feel that people in Coco Hill are more prosperous; the majority of white-collar workers reside there and the latter tend to look with disdain on Cane Road. However, poor persons who live on a main road or in Coco Hill do not receive additional status from their residential location, while big farmers, entrepreneurs, and white-collar workers living in the bush or in Cane Road, who have built relatively modern homes and maintain a life style associated with their respective status groups, are not respected less than their peers in Coco Hill.

Age and sex, unlike most of the other criteria discussed, are ascribed characteristics. They are important in defining authority within the family, but are of minimal importance in community-wide status differentiation. An older person is usually treated with some degree of deference by young people, but if he is poor and can no longer perform any useful functions, he is not held in high esteem. This is more true of elderly men than women, since old women can still act in useful roles such as caring for grandchildren. Very old men can no longer even hope to carry out the breadwinning functions expected of men in Jamaican society. The old men respected in the community are those who have been financially successful, leaders in the churches and voluntary associations, and substantial landowners. Aging, rather than age itself, is the basis of prestige, because it provides the opportunity to accumulate material goods, to become successful in an occupation, and to establish durable social ties.

There is a clear-cut division of labor between men and women. Men work in the fields, hire themselves out as agricultural and road laborers, work at the local factories and bauxite companies, and occupy most of the official positions in local associations and churches. Women's domain, on the other hand, is the home. Although some do work in the fields, concentrating on lighter tasks such as weeding, most merely cultivate subsistence garden plots.* There are some typical female occupations—higglering, domestic work, clerical work in the post office, and teaching. Although women receive deference within the family because they fill valued childrearing roles as mothers, grand-mothers, and aunts, within the community their status depends on the usual objective criteria. In the survey, about 75 per cent of those named as respected were men. The women listed included teachers, shop-keepers, clerks, and the Post Mistress.

SUBJECTIVE RANKING

When I asked the villagers to rank themselves, rather than their neighbors, they referred not to their local status but to their position in the island-wide system of stratification. Most villagers conceive of this system as one made up of three classes, upper, middle, and lower; nearly all ranked themselves at the bottom of this hierarchy. One of

* The following figures on the occupations of adult females on Percy Road indicate the extent to which women engage in farming: full-time, 10 per cent; housekeepers and some farming, 24 per cent; farmers and other occupations, 16 per cent; non-farmers, 50 per cent.

the poorest women in the community, a black woman who lives in a
one-room shack in the bush and who works out as a domestic, told me:

> All different classes, all the same, but rough is three. You have the
> opposite sets—those are the higher class, the white folks. You have
> the medium, the set with the rich. Those people can balance them-
> self as they like and they are not so rich as the top class. And then
> you have a poor set. I are the lower class, brother, the poorest class.

A higgler, the wife of a carpenter/farmer who owned two acres of
land and lived in a new, fairly modern home explained:

> Divided up with rich and poor and there is some in-between, not so
> bad. Rich ones have the monies such as Mr. Cooper [white estate
> owner]. One in the middle, can only find themselves a little thing.
> Maybe able to buy a little easier than some. Poor ones, like me.
> Don't am I poor? Yes man! I am poor. Is just from the good mind
> and the ambitious that I build this house. For I had to borrow the
> money to make it.

Finally, the wife of a big farmer told me:

> Well, you have the lower income, middle, and higher. The lower
> income are the poor, poor ones. I would classify myself in the
> lower one. The middle, they are not really rich but they are more
> independent. The teacher or a nurse whose husband is in good
> position can buy a good dress or have a chicken for dinner. The
> higher ones, the rich people. Like this man McNeil [fair-skinned
> estate owner]. He has something to buy and spare. Here right now
> and the children need the clothes and I need a dress and days we
> would like a chicken and don't have the money to buy it. The
> wealthy can buy and spare. The majority in Coco Hill is the low
> income people.

In general, the upper classes are thought to be employers, rich,
white, and independent. The middle classes are felt to occupy salaried,
nonagricultural positions, and to have enough money to maintain a
desired life style. The villagers stressed that members of the middle
class did not engage in agricultural work. Members of the poorer class
are identified as farmers or laborers who could not afford to maintain a
"respectable" style of life.

Nearly everyone in the community ranked himself as a member of
the lower class. On Percy Road all but the white-collar workers and
two of the largest shopowners told me that they were poor and lower
class. One big farmer told me, "Most people don't think the farmer is a
respectable people." Yet this man is one of the most successful farmers
in the district, owns 15 acres of land, is the president of the Jamaica
Agricultural Society, an officer in three other voluntary associations, a

deacon of his church, and father of two university-educated children.

This is not to say that people in the village are unaware of their place in the local status hierarchy; many receive prestige from their positions in the local community. While some small farmers and wage laborers told me, "I don't think there is any poorer than me so," many of the more successful farmers explained, when I specifically asked them about their rank in the village, that there were many others worse off than they. For example, the wife of the big farmer quoted above said, "You have people worse than me. Poorer than me still. I think God is good and great because there are still some who are worse. There are some can't find a quarter pound of salt fish and I have a pound of beef."

LOCAL AND NATIONAL STATUS SYSTEMS

Status in Coco Hill appears to be defined by two different sets of standards, one referring primarily to the local community and the other to the national society. How are they related to each other? Do they perhaps represent one underlying status system? What are their common features? In what ways are they distinctive?

Basically, the status distinctions in Coco Hill reflect those of the entire island; variations between the two represent local elaborations on the larger society's status system. Both locally and nationally, the basic criteria for defining status are occupation, land ownership, income, and life style. These are important in Coco Hill precisely because they are associated with high rank in the national society. Although I prefer to speak of status rather than deference systems—individuals may seem to defer to those in higher positions, but they often harbor resentment toward them, which may at times be expressed openly—this analysis supports Edward Shils' contention that local and national deference systems are not in conflict with one another, and "local differentiations are often simply refined applications of perceptions of evaluations which have the centre as the point of reference." * Furthermore, as Shils

* Edward Shils, "Deference," in *Social Stratification*, ed. J. A. Jackson (Cambridge: Cambridge University Press, 1968), p. 129. This is in contrast to M. G. Smith's plural society theory. According to the plural society model, Jamaican society consists of three separate cultural and social sections: white (European culture); black (African culture and locally developed culture); brown (a mixture of patterns from both of these groups). Order in the society is achieved only through the regulation of intersectional relations by the power and force imposed by the dominant, though minority, section. Each section is characterized by its own family, kinship, and mating system, its own religious beliefs and practices, socialization system, recreational activities, values, and language variant. Following this theory, each section has a self-contained system of stratification with its own criteria for determining prestige. M. G. Smith's theoretical formulations are clearly set out in a number of articles which have been published in M. G. Smith, *op. cit.* For criticisms of this model see: Lloyd Braithwaite, "Social Stratification and

writes, local deference systems appear more differentiated to those who participate in them than do the national systems which they experience less directly. Individuals are more sensitive to finer gradations of status within Coco Hill than in the national society; they perceive the local status system in more personal terms. Thus, when the villagers talked about status differentiation in Coco Hill, they cited specific individuals, whereas in speaking of the whole society they tended to refer to categories such as "we the poorer class" and "up class people them." Many villagers also stressed the moral or behavioral attributes of those they respected in the community, attributes of which they would have been aware through personal encounters.

Color and education, though important in the villagers' conception of the island's hierarchy, were rarely mentioned in describing local status. Within Coco Hill, color and educational attainment are not significant differentiating criteria; most of the villagers are black and have had little schooling. However, within Jamaican society, occupational and status differences closely parallel educational and color distinctions. The middle and upper classes are still predominantly white and colored, the lower classes overwhelmingly black. This correlation is recognized by Coco Hill residents, particularly wage laborers and less successful small farmers, who most frequently identify the upper classes in Jamaica as white and the lower classes as black. It is also not surprising that many in Coco Hill associate education with high rank in the national society, since it is the main channel for occupational mobility; the majority of the island's middle class have qualified for their occupations by successfully completing examinations or by graduating from secondary school, training colleges, or university.

CONCLUSION

The position a villager occupies in the local status hierarchy is important in determining everyday activities and relationships. Rank in the local status system is not the only factor which shapes social relations in the community; ties of kinship, residence, and association

Cultural Pluralism," in *Social and Cultural Pluralism in the Caribbean,* ed. Vera Rubin (New York: Annals of the New York Academy of Sciences, 1960), pp. 816–831; R. S. Bryce-Laporte, "M. G. Smith's Version of Pluralism: The Questions It Raises," *Comparative Studies in Society and History,* X (October, 1967), 114–120; Malcolm Cross, "Cultural Pluralism and Sociological Theory: A Critique and Reevaluation," *Social and Economic Studies,* XVII (December, 1968), 381–397; H. I. McKenzie, "The Plural Society Debate: Some Comments on a Recent Contribution," *Social and Economic Studies,* XV (March, 1966), 53–60; Vera Rubin, "Social and Cultural Pluralism by M. G. Smith," in *Social and Cultural Pluralism in the Caribbean,* pp. 780–785; R. T. Smith, review of *Social and Cultural Pluralism in the Caribbean* in *American Anthropologist,* LXIII (February, 1961), 155–157; R. T. Smith, "People and Change," *New World: Guyana Independence Issue* (Demerara, Guyana: May, 1966), pp. 49–54.

membership, for example, are also important, but a villager's local status position is a major factor in shaping his behavior and attitudes. At the same time, the villagers occupy status positions in the island-wide system of stratification; it is this national system which structures the goals they strive to achieve, and affects the legitimate means available to them for attaining these goals. The villagers desire to improve their own or their children's status in the national society, and this aim has far-reaching consequences in their lives.

PART 2

Education

III

History of Education in Jamaica

As recently as a generation ago a visitor to rural Jamaica would not have found the same enthusiasm for education that flourishes today. Why have educational values and opportunities changed in this time? Did the system of formal education serve different functions in the past than it does now? What was the ideological framework underlying this system, and what has been the nature of recent ideological and structural changes in the educational system?

Since the end of the nineteenth century the system of formal education has served two major functions in Jamaican society. First, rural Jamaicans are taught in school to respect existing social, economic, and political institutions, and learn that high-ranking positions within these are achieved by following certain occupations and life styles and acquiring particular cultural characteristics. Thus educational institutions function to motivate aspirations for mobility and to disseminate a set of goals to the population.

Second, the educational system provides the principal means for achieving mobility. Occupation has long been a primary basis of social identity in Jamaica and a focus of the island-wide system of stratification; it has been the secondary schools which provide individuals with the skills necessary to qualify for prestigious and well-paid jobs. As the established route to occupational advancement and the acquisition of desirable cultural characteristics, education came to have its own symbolic significance and to be a basis for prestige in itself.

INSPIRATIONS FOR MOBILITY IN THE PAST

Even in the slavery period, educational institutions served to disseminate a set of values and goals to the population. Although the slaves received no formal education, foreign missionaries ran church schools on some of the plantations in the hope of bringing civilization to the heathen and providing the slaves with some of the spiritual comforts of Christianity.* In order to overcome the resistance of the planters, who feared that religious teachings would arouse discontent among their slaves, the missionaries stressed the virtue of submission and the moral superiority of whites, principles which they too no doubt believed.

More important, the plantation itself became, according to Raymond Smith, a "peculiar kind of instrument for the re-socialization of those who fell within its sphere of influence." [1] Smith suggests that the plantation had many features of a "total institution"—regimentation under a small staff, for example—which, as a rule, induced the slaves to accept the putative superiority of English planters and estate managers and their own inferior status. However, an internal ranking system also developed. Occupation was the primary basis for differentiation, but high status also came to be associated with English culture and ancestry, as well as light skin. The need for house servants, overseers, and craftsmen provided some slaves with the opportunity for better treatment, freedom, and prestige. Those slaves preferred by whites were creole slaves, born in Jamaica, and light-skinned slaves, offspring of black women and European men. This differentiation furthered cultural distinctions among the slaves. A house slave or craftsman, for example, had more opportunity than a field hand to interact with whites on an informal basis, and was often taught to read and write. Slaves of higher status regarded themselves as superior to field hands and, for the most part, this superiority was acknowledged by their fellow slaves because, in addition to their prestigious occupations, the former more closely approximated the customs, speech, and manners of their masters.

After the abolition of slavery in 1838, the British laid the ground-

---

* In 1754, four Moravian missionaries came to the island from England. They were followed by the Methodists in 1789, the Scottish Missionary Society in 1800, and English Baptists in 1814. American Negroes, brought to the island by loyalist families from the United States, formed the Baptist Church in 1784.

work for the formal system of education.* Between 1837 and 1846 the British government gave annual education grants to the Jamaican Assembly. However, the Assembly made no attempt to set up its own educational system and allocated the grants to religious missions. With the establishment of Crown Colony government in 1866, the power of the Governor greatly increased. One outcome of this change was a more active interest in the education of ex-slaves. Denominational schools were maintained, but they were placed under the supervision of an official inspectorate. In 1885 the government began to build public primary schools and in 1892 school fees, which had ranged from 1½ to six pence a week, were abolished.

Why was the colonial government interested in supporting a system of primary education? Education was a major tool in the government's deliberate attempt to integrate ex-slaves into colonial society as a basis for social order. Although the planters were initially alarmed at the spread of education to the ex-slaves, they were soon convinced that such training would make for a peaceful and contented lower class. Moreover, they tolerated the spending of colony funds for this purpose in exchange for British recognition of the need to maintain plantation agriculture.

These aims are made clear in a report by a British minister sent to the West Indies to investigate social conditions during the apprenticeship period, immediately following the abolition Act of 1833:

> The peace and prosperity of the Empire at large may be not remotely influenced by their moral condition; . . . [the ex-slaves'] performance of the functions of a labouring class in a civilised community will depend entirely on the power over their minds of the same prudential and moral motives which govern more or less

---

* After emancipation many slaves formed independent settlements in the inland mountainous regions of the island. The sugar economy occupied only a small part of the island, the flat areas along the coast—the hilly regions further inland were largely undeveloped. With emancipation, the unoccupied land was open to settlement by purchase, rent, or squatting. According to Hugh Paget, many ex-slaves would have preferred to remain in their old villages on the estates and to save enough money to purchase their huts and gardens. However, because of the high rents charged by the planters, the fear of eviction, and the availability of land in the hills for settlement, many left the estates. Hugh Paget, "The Free Village System in Jamaica," *Caribbean Quarterly*, X (March, 1964), 43. The missionaries, in particular the Baptists, played an important role in the movement toward independent land ownership. The Baptists purchased land in various parts of the island and by 1842 had established 150–200 free villages. The new settlers grew crops for subsistence and internal markets and earned cash by working out at the estates. For a more detailed discussion of Jamaican society at this time see Douglas Hall, *Free Jamaica, 1838–1865, An Economic History* (New Haven: Yale University Press, 1959).

the mass of the people here. If they are not so disposed as to fulfil these functions, property will perish in the colonies for lack of human impulsion; the whites will no longer reside there; and the liberated negroes themselves will probably cease to be progressive. The law having already determined and enforced their civic rights, the task of bettering their condition can be advanced only by education.[2]

In the primary schools the children of the ex-slaves were taught to respect the superiority of the English and local white elite because of the latter's culture and color:

> there was . . . a deliberate attempt to create a set of common values, or an ideology, for the whole society. These values stressed the importance of christianity, of education, respect of the law, "good" as opposed to "rough" or "bad" behaviour, the need for moral upliftment, and the importance of using proper language; all factors which emphasized not only the *de facto* power of the Europeans but also the superiority of English culture.[3]

The schools were not the only institutions through which these values were disseminated. Churches and courts were also important; a network of Christian churches, formed by British missionaries who had been active before emancipation, spread throughout the entire island, and the rural population was subject to the island-wide legal system.

The rural villagers generally came to respect the moral and cultural superiority of things English, and desired to adopt these ways whenever possible. Those who went to primary school * learned there that the "admirable man" [4] followed a life style similar to that of the English elite, was white—or light skinned—and had acquired English cultural traits. They were taught that this image could be attained, at least in part, by success in the educational system, which would provide them with occupational skills and the ability to speak and act "properly." ** This was tempered by the idea that as descendants of

---

* Percentage of Children of School Age (5–14) Enrolled in School:

    1881   45.9 per cent
    1891   60.7 per cent
    1911   58.0 per cent
    1921   57.3 per cent

Eisner, *op. cit.*, p. 335.

** It is beyond the scope of this study to explain why most rural villagers did not, and still do not, conform to many dominant cultural traditions, even though they recognize that these traditions are associated with high status in the society. In terms of acquiring certain speech patterns associated with the white elite, I suggest that several complex factors must be considered. Children of rural settlers received poor training in primary schools, and the majority did not attend classes regularly. Thus their opportunities to learn correct forms of speech were limited. Even if they did begin to acquire these correct speech patterns, old and common

black farmers they were best suited to agricultural work, and that only a few exceptional children could succeed in the educational system and advance occupationally.

PAST AVENUES FOR OCCUPATIONAL MOBILITY

Occupation has long been not only a source of social identity but also a crucial basis for ranking in Jamaican society. This stems from Jamaica's past history as a plantation society. Plantations dominated the island's economy from the eighteenth century to the 1950's:

> The plantation was more than a market place in which people met to exchange goods and services, . . . *it was the initial framework for a system of graded occupational categories.* Whereas in parts of Africa, for example, one might be able to think of a tribal population being drawn into an occupational system from which they might periodically or permanently withdraw, *occupation in the Caribbean is a primary social identity.* Terms such as "small farmer," "rice farmer," or "cane farmer" are usually more appropriate than "peasant," for farming is an occupation rather than a way of life.[5] [italics mine]

Because the formal educational institutions taught individuals the skills necessary to qualify for desired occupational roles, they provided the major channel for upward mobility. However, the type of education—secondary or university—needed for these occupations was first formally and then informally restricted to the island's relatively small middle and upper classes.

Before emancipation, slaves were legally barred from attending the island's privately endowed schools. These schools, which trained students in academic subjects, catered to the children of whites and free persons of color. Founded in the eighteenth century by wealthy planters and merchants, they were designed to provide an education

---

forms were reinforced by their regular interactions with persons who did not speak "properly." Moreover, a black farmer who spoke in the manner of the white elite was felt to be assuming an unwarranted superiority. Negative sanctions discouraged him from speaking in this way and thereby acting "haughty," "proud," and "presumptuous." He might be the butt of local rumor and ridicule, and he might lose the reciprocity of kin and neighbors. In addition, he might not be employed by the white-collar workers and planters in the district or receive favors from them, because they resented his "arrogant" behavior. In contrast, it was acceptable—and, indeed expected—that a person who altered his occupational status and became, for example, a professional or a civil servant, would acquire English speech patterns. He no longer associated on an equal basis with poor, black farmers but instead with others in his new status position. This tended to reinforce the newly acquired speech patterns. He trained his children to speak in this manner and castigated them if they resorted to "common" speech.

for children who could not afford to go "home" to England to school
and they were usually small, with about 10 pupils each.

The free persons of color sought education for two main reasons:
to qualify for prestigious and remunerative occupations, and to establish their equality with whites. Those who could afford to sent their
children to England to be educated, as wealthy white planters did.
This expense was within the means of only a few free persons of color;
most other successful members of this group sent their children to one
of the island's privately endowed schools.

As products of unions between slaves and white men, the free
persons of color held an ambiguous position in slave society. They
wanted to distinguish themselves from the mass of blacks, and be
treated like whites, but until the 1830's there were numerous restrictions on their civil rights. For example, they could inherit only a limited
amount of property, could not be elected to the Assembly or vote in
elections, and they could not give evidence in the courts of law. Even
so, a few entered the professions, many went into business, and despite
the laws which were designed to keep them from owning property,
some acquired considerable wealth. By the 1830's they outnumbered
the whites; in 1834 there were approximately 45,000 free persons of
color, 15,000 whites, and 311,100 slaves in Jamaica.

For several reasons, free persons of color were rarely successful in
plantation agriculture. To become great planters was beyond their
resources and if they attempted to set up as independent small planters,
they were "likely to be defeated by a combination of the disadvantages
of their class and the disadvantages that had already virtually wiped
out the small white planter . . . small planters had . . . experienced
the extreme difficulty of competing with them [large planters] for the
land, labour, and credit needed for survival. The free man of colour,
who had even less access to mercantile credit and connections than the
poorer whites, had little hope of succeeding where the whites had
failed." [6] They were kept out of supervisory posts on the estates by the
financial penalties imposed by deficiency laws on planters who failed
to employ a fixed number of whites in proportion to the number of
slaves. Since they were reluctant to labor for themselves in the fields
but used slaves for this purpose, "the prospects of subsistence farming
on this basis were unpromising. . . . If the free coloured attempted to
make a living instead by producing food for sale in the internal markets
. . . they had to encounter the formidable competition of the slaves,
who were already well established in this trade." [7] The majority of free
persons of color thus sought advancement in towns, which offered
greater opportunities for free labor than did the rural areas with their

slave plantations. They became tradesmen, shopkeepers, and clerks in merchant houses.

Free persons of color used education to enhance their status in Jamaican society. One of their major arguments in the fight to remove the legal disabilities imposed on them was that they had attained a high educational level and a "civilized" standard of living. However, even after these disabilities were removed—in 1813 property inheritance restrictions were lifted and in 1830 free persons of color were given the right to hold public office and to vote—they were not regarded as equals by the whites. In school, the free coloreds sought an academic training which emphasized classical subjects. Clearly such training was not necessary for the jobs available in the society—a clerk or tradesman or even a journalist did not need to know Greek or Latin or many of the other subjects which were taught in the private schools. However, proficiency in these subjects provided them with a claim to status and possible preferment for the few prestigious civil service and professional posts available; an individual who knew Latin, Greek, and philosophy, would, it was hoped, be deemed worthy and able by the whites.*

It was not until the end of the nineteenth century that the secondary school system began to expand. At this time a need developed to fill certain intermediate occupational positions with Jamaicans, since fewer Englishmen were coming to the island to occupy low-level professional and civil service posts. Moreover, the Colonial Office required personnel for its newly instituted welfare programs. This stimulated the expansion of the secondary school system and the creation of government scholarships for university education abroad. It also provided some opportunities for occupational advancement, but for the bulk of the population, opportunities for occupational mobility through education were still very limited.

An important factor in the survival of limitations on mobility was

* The desire to gain the acceptance of whites also promoted conspicuous consumption among free persons of color and militated against their saving for investment in agriculture and business—for example, George William Gordon, who by 1843 had built up a business worth £10,000, used a considerable portion of his savings to send his sisters to England and France to be educated. Many free persons of color spent vast sums on servants and entertaining lavishly.

It was new immigrant groups, first Jews, then Syrians and Chinese, rather than the creole elite, who came to dominate the mercantile establishments of the island. Lloyd Braithwaite describes the similar success of the Portuguese and Syrians in shopkeeping and dry goods in Trinidad, pointing out that "precisely because they did not share the same scale of values, they were able to accumulate wealth with greater ease than the local population who were committed to the 'standards of living' and the symbolism of their respective classes." Lloyd Braithwaite, "Social Stratification in Trinidad," *Social and Economic Studies*, II (October, 1953), 49.

the Colonial Office's continued recognition of the need to maintain plantation agriculture. Those charged with planning educational programs did not want to "spoil" the settlers (ex-slaves and their descendants) for agricultural labor on the estates. They did not design the programs to provide the settlers with opportunities for advancement, but merely wished to teach them the rudiments of reading and writing and to make them a "civilized" lower class.

Limited opportunities for educational advances by the rural settlers were justified and reinforced by an elaborate ideology. On the one hand, the colonial government had institutionalized the idea that persons should advance according to their ability. Avenues for educational, and therefore, occupational mobility were theoretically open to individuals of all classes and colors. On the other hand, the ruling elite believed that each racial group had aptitudes for different types of occupations [8] and informally restricted access to education. The Colonial Office intended secondary education to benefit the island's white and colored citizens. It was felt that whites were best suited to the top political, administrative, and economic positions, persons of color for occupations of intermediate status, such as teaching and low-level civil service posts, and blacks for agricultural work and other low-status occupations.*

The Colonial Office and the local elites thus sought to promote agricultural and industrial, rather than academic, training among the ex-slaves; but, the settlers did not desire agricultural training. As Philip Foster notes in his study of education in Ghana:

> Education, in practice, was valued for its cash return, and it remained virtually the only mode by which individuals could partially dissociate themselves from traditional society and enter the small but relatively lucrative number of posts then open to Africans . . . parents did not send their children to school so that they could return to subsistence agricultural activities, even if the schools provided courses of agricultural training. Education meant one thing above all, the opportunity to enter more highly paid posts within the exchange sector of the economy.**

---

* In fact, members of the lower class were defined as black even if they were light skinned.

** Philip Foster, *Education and Social Change in Ghana* (Chicago: University of Chicago Press, 1965), pp. 64–66. The function of education was essentially similar in the two societies even though in Jamaica, unlike Ghana, there had been no tribal groups. In Ghana, education served as the gateway to new occupational roles which provided an *alternative* avenue of mobility, independent of tribal modes of status acquisition. In Jamaican society no such alternatives existed. There was one system of graded occupational categories and the ex-slaves, as estate laborers and semi-subsistence cultivators, ranked at the bottom of this system.

However, in Jamaica, the type of education needed for the highly paid posts Foster mentions, secondary education, remained limited to a small percentage of the island's population. As late as 1929, secondary school education was available to about one school child in 50. Until recently, only a few rural children managed to win scholarships to secondary school.* Access to secondary education depended upon the parents' ability to pay fees or the children's ability to win scholarships; it was very difficult for a child to win a scholarship after attending an inferior government primary school. The major means of advancement for children from lower-class families was through the teaching profession. One could qualify for primary school teaching by serving as a pupil teacher, or monitor, in a local school and eventually passing teacher certificate examinations. While this system provided a degree of mobility for members of the lower class, usually children of shopkeepers, tradesmen, and more prosperous farmers, it lowered the standards of the primary schools and further reduced chances for children who attended them to win scholarships to secondary school.

Understandably, the rural villagers became disillusioned with education—"parents became less keen on an education that did not fit their children for . . . the social advancement they had hoped for." [9]

Were other avenues of mobility open to the rural population? After emancipation there was more occupational differentiation in the society. The plantations had traditionally provided slaves with medical care, housing, and clothing. With the abolition of slavery, the slave population became wage earners and consumers; this stimulated the growth of a small shopkeeping class in the countryside and a merchant class in the towns. However, as Raymond Smith notes, ". . . the really profitable import–export and wholesale trade was dominated by a class of merchant planters, while at the bottom the proliferation of small shops kept growth limited." [10]

As for opportunities in agriculture,[11] some settlers were able to accumulate considerable amounts of land, in a few cases over 500 acres, but even these successful farmers could not compete with estate owners, who monopolized much of the best land on the island. In any case, most small settlers did not have the cash or credit to expand their land holdings significantly.

RECENT DEVELOPMENTS AND IDEOLOGICAL CHANGES

Since the end of World War II, and especially since independence in 1962, there have been a number of changes, particularly in the

* The first scholarships to children from public primary schools were awarded in the 1890's.

island's system of formal education, which have increased upward mobility. Educational programs are important in the platforms of both major political parties, and the party in power has sought to expand and democratize the educational institutions of the society. The government sees education as an area in which tangible progress can be demonstrated; the amount of money spent on education or the number of schools built are evidence of efforts to create a better and more egalitarian society. Moreover, Jamaican leaders desire to prove, by raising literacy rates and educational standards, that Jamaica is equal to older nations and is no longer backward or underdeveloped.[12]

One noteworthy change has been a shift in the ideological framework which supports the educational system. Implicit in the ideologies of the new elites are two long-held conceptions: not everyone can succeed in the educational system; those who do succeed are worthy of respect, because in a society without formal restrictions on entering university or secondary school, success is based on ability. Political elites have never proposed making secondary or university education available to all. What is new is the claim that they will provide equal opportunities for children from all classes to compete for the limited number of places available. This conception of equality is clearly stated by the then-leader of the Opposition, Michael Manley:

> By equality, I do not mean that everyone should get the same wages regardless of the work performed or that all people have the same tastes or ability. What I mean is that the society must be so designed to ensure, so far as human ingenuity can provide, every man will start with an equal chance. This derives in turn from the belief that men are born equal in the sense that they are born with an equal attainment to a chance . . . . An egalitarian system must rest upon the possession by every man of the minimum means of self-support, the economic security without which family life is impossible, a decent home without which life is insupportable, and an educational system that puts all the children in one stream where they can compete equally for the benefits of the educational system.[13]

The political leaders do not deny that occupations are ranked in Jamaican society, or that education provides legitimate access to positions of prestige, power, and influence. A speech by the Minister of Education to the students at a prestigious secondary school on the island expresses these ideas:

> The educational policies of the present government were designed to give citizens an opportunity to occupy the highest, most lucrative, dignified and influential positions in the land. The reaching

of these levels, however, depends on your ability and personality
. . . . If I felt that the educational policies I am implementing
meant that because the father of a child is a cane cutter or a street
sweeper that that child must aim at rising no higher than a cane
cutter or street sweeper, I would resign immediately. . . . Not
that I disrespect cane cutters and street sweepers. I respect those
persons but the educational system must provide for the children
of the poorest parentage to become the great members of the
society.[14]

While he emphasizes that equal opportunities are available to all,
the Minister also implies that individuals in certain occupations are
less worthy of respect than those who have succeeded in the educational system. Education is viewed as the legitimate means to attain
dignity, wealth, and influence.

As for actual changes, various programs have been instituted to
equalize access to education. The quality of primary education has
been improved, and the number of secondary school scholarships
available to children from government primary schools increased.
Statistics quoted by government officials show a marked rise in literacy
over the past 20 years: in 1943, 23.9 per cent of the population 10
years and older were illiterate, compared with 15.1 per cent in 1960.
School attendance has also increased: 39.15 per cent of those between
the ages of five and 24 attended school in 1943, 53.15 per cent in 1960.
Moreover, 6.6 per cent of the population 15 and older had attended
secondary school in 1960 as opposed to 3.5 per cent in 1943.[15]

A major emphasis in educational planning is on the lower levels
of the educational system. The government has built more primary
school buildings, increased the West Indian content of curricula, and
instituted a program to staff the primary schools with only college-
trained teachers. It has also developed government-supported basic
schools, that is, schools for children under six.

The most publicized program in recent years has been the development of junior secondary schools.* These schools are designed to
provide advanced training for those who do not qualify for secondary
school. Through the junior secondary schools, the government hopes
to keep a significant proportion of young people out of the labor force
until they are older and have acquired some skill, as well as to satisfy
the increasing demands of the population for more educational opportunities. The government has also expanded its vocational training

* Junior secondary schools, unlike regular secondary schools, have no admissions tests and provide candidates for secondary schools and advanced technical
schools. Throughout the book secondary education refers to academic secondary
education.

programs: a number of home-craft centers, to train girls for domestic employment, and youth camps, to train boys for trades, have been built.

As for secondary education, the government has increased the number of scholarships available to secondary schools and has taken measures to correct the biases in selection which favored the children of better-off parents. Children in the primary schools who wish to attend secondary school are awarded free places or scholarships on the basis of their performance on the Common Entrance Examination. Under a new government regulation, the bulk of the scholarships must be given to children from government primary schools rather than from the private preparatory schools which can afford to train their pupils more efficiently. However, the government has not built any new academic secondary schools, leaving the field to those in existence. There are 42 secondary schools which are grant-aided by the government. Since 1957 five new technical high schools have been built, bringing the total to six.

The Jamaica School Certificate Examinations have recently replaced the Jamaica Local Examinations.* The latter provided rural villagers with the principal avenue for occupational mobility in colonial society. A student who passed the Jamaica Locals could become a primary school teacher, low-grade civil servant, or enter a training college. The Jamaica School Certificate Examinations qualify students for the same occupations and training colleges but they are somewhat easier than the Jamaica Locals and can be taken after an individual leaves primary school.

Higher education has also expanded in recent years and has provided new opportunities for children from poor families to attend university or college. It is no longer neecssary to go abroad to university—the main branch of the University of the West Indies is located in Kingston, as is the College of Arts, Science and Technology. The teacher training colleges, nursing schools, and the Jamaica School of Agriculture have also expanded their capacities.

The conception of what constitutes a good education is still basically traditional. The subjects taught in primary school are English grammar and literature, English history, Bible knowledge, needlework, art, music, mathematics, home economics, and physical education. Although there have been concerted attempts to "West-Indianize" the curriculum, with the addition of West Indian history, geography, and

---

* The Jamaica School Certificate Examinations are not to be confused with the Common Entrance Examination. The latter are taken by students when they are 11 plus and qualify them for free places in secondary school. The Jamaica School Certificate Examinations are taken when the students are older and qualify them for certain jobs.

literature, many children still learn to read from books prepared for English schools, illustrated with pictures of English wheatfields and well-clad English children. Where these have been replaced by West Indian texts, they usually picture light-skinned children in middle-class environments. Portraits of the Queen of England still hang on the walls of many primary schools; in music class, the children learn songs about snow and animals that they probably will never see.

There has been some shift toward the teaching of technical subjects. The emphasis in primary schools is, however, still on academic rather than basic industrial training. This is related not only to the formal requirements of the educational system but to the occupational opportunities available. Technical occupations enjoy greater prestige than they did a decade or two ago; they may lead to jobs in the burgeoning bauxite, construction, and service industries, which pay the high salaries necessary to support desired life styles. But the best jobs in these fields require at least a technical high school education, and often, as in engineering, university training. To qualify for admission to schools which provide this training, a student must pass island-wide examinations in academic as well as technical subjects. Opportunities for women are more limited. They are informally excluded from technical occupations. They aim instead to become secretaries, clerks, teachers, and nurses, and for these jobs an academic education is required. The preoccupation with academic education is, then, not merely an inheritance from past mobility patterns, but a reflection of current occupational opportunities.

The idea that certain groups in the society are better suited for different occupations lingers in modern Jamaica. As the Colonial Office and the white planter elite stressed the need for agricultural training in the schools, so too, new political leaders continue to harp on this theme. There are numerous proposals for introducing agriculture into the primary schools, and to encourage school leavers—implicitly, lower-class, rural, black school leavers who have not proved competent on examinations—to take up agricultural occupations, which most will probably do anyway. Since schooling is desired precisely in order to qualify for nonagricultural occupations, few Jamaicans are enthusiastic about agricultural education at the primary level.

CONCLUSION

Basically the Jamaican system of formal education continues to serve the same functions that it has for nearly a century. Primary schools play a major role in disseminating societal goals and values to the bulk of the population; secondary schools provide the major

avenue to occupational mobility. However, recent changes in the
structure of the educational system, although limited, have provided
lower-class Jamaicans with new opportunities. Education has always
been an important basis for status differentiation in Jamaican society,
and with the opening up of opportunities for lower-class children, it
is becoming one of the most important status-defining criteria in the
society.*

* Raymond Smith observes that the new elites may well become a meritocracy.
See Smith, "Social Stratification in the Caribbean," p. 57. Corresponding changes
in the political system have minimized the importance of color as a basis for status
differentiation. Top administrative and political posts are now held by black and
colored Jamaicans; a black person who receives a good education, lives in a nice
home, and so on, can qualify for high status in the society.

IV

Education and
Status Aspirations

To understand social mobility and the new mobility opportunities available to Coco Hill residents, it is important to know the role education plays in their lives and in their children's lives.

ATTITUDES TOWARD EDUCATION

The villagers of Coco Hill feel that education is the key means to success in Jamaican society and that increased opportunities to attend secondary school represent the most significant change for the better in recent years. These attitudes are clearly shown in the sample survey of 40 adult household heads taken in the summer of 1968. The respondents—22 small farmers, eight wage laborers, five white-collar workers, and five big farmers—were interviewed in order to locate potential informants for the kinship project in which I was involved.* The following questions relate to this study:

* This was a study of Comparative Family Structure directed by Professor Raymond T. Smith of the University of Chicago and financed by a grant from the National Science Foundation CS 1709. The questionnaire used was adapted from the Guyana survey of Education and Social Mobility carried out by Raymond T. Smith and Sara Graham.

1. Do you think that there is more opportunity for people to get ahead in Jamaica today than there was 20 years ago?
2. Why do you think this is so?
3. What would you say is the most important way of getting ahead in Jamaica today?
4. Why do you think this is so?
5. What sort of people do you think are the most highly regarded in Jamaica today?
6. Why do you think this is so?
7. What sort of people do you think are the most poorly regarded in Jamaica today?
8. Why do you think this is so?

The overwhelming response to the first question was yes. Thirty-five individuals felt that there was more opportunity today than 20 years ago; five—four wage laborers and one small farmer—said no. The majority of those who answered in the affirmative felt that this increased opportunity was due to the spread of education. Education was deemed the most important way of advancing by over 75 per cent of the respondents. Respondents also felt that the most highly regarded people were educated persons, whites, and foreigners. The reasons for this were diverse. However, most of the responses reflected the belief that the educated, the whites, and the foreigners were financially independent. They were also viewed as more intelligent, more respectable, and as looked up to by other people. In contrast, those who were looked down upon were farmers, blacks, people who didn't work, and the uneducated. Again, the reasons for giving this answer were varied. The majority felt that people were poorly regarded because they had no money. Others explained that "they come in dirty from the fields . . . they can't get anything to do . . . they can't get ahead."

EDUCATION AND MOBILITY

The villagers rightly perceive that education is the most likely way to alter their social status. Entrepreneurial opportunities for them are limited by the difficulty of securing capital. And, since cash yields from local enterprises are usually low, the entrepreneur can rarely alter his status in the national society. Furthermore, these businesses are often risky and they involve long working hours. Nor is it realistic for individuals in Coco Hill, as in the society generally, to seek social mobility through farming. In recent years, opportunities for land expansion have decreased markedly in St. Ann. In addition to the population increase and soil erosion—problems common to all parts of the island—the bauxite companies have displaced hundreds of farmers in some sections of the parish. The tourist industry has taken up much of the available land on the north coast and has caused prices of the remaining farms to soar. Estates and large properties monopolize huge tracts of the best land in the parish. Furthermore, even if a man could accumulate the cash to purchase 15 acres of land, a relatively large amount by standards in Coco Hill, income from his land would not enable him to follow the popularly desired life style. To do this, he would need at least 50 acres, an unrealistic goal for most of the villagers. The main avenue for social mobility therefore is entry into prestigious and well-paid public service or commercial jobs.

Through reports in the newspapers and on the radio, sermons in the churches, and talks by school teachers and other local leaders, the importance of education filters down to the village level. For example, at a meeting of 50 members of the local Parent-Teacher Association, the Head Teacher in Coco Hill exhorted parents to send their children to school. He stressed that education was the way to become a respected member of the society and that many children in the community had "untapped" educational potential:

> If you don't take an interest in education now, that same boy will not be able to earn a decent living because he is not skilled. Today you must be able to read and write intelligently. We have passed to a technological age. We are to educate people for life, in order to live, to contribute. The world calls for that now. Everyone can be trained into something useful. Even to do ordinary laboring at bauxite you have to pass a test [this is true for Kaiser Bauxite Company]. Even if you want to go to the United States, you can't go unless you can read and write [this is not true]. Try to live in this day and age. Children were not born to stay home and work and carry water. When school time comes, they must down the water and come to school. Don't throw away a child at 16 because they can't make life. Some barristers don't go 'til them 45. What we aim is to inject some pride in our country. If we can't do our job well, is a man who feels a sense of well-being and has contributed something to his country. We want people to rise to perform all the jobs this country needs. Who knows if tomorrow we don't have a Prime Minister from Coco Hill? We have to take an interest in our children.

CHANGING PATTERNS

The villagers of Coco Hill have not always been eager to send their children to school. The wife of the former Head Teacher explained the difficulties that she and her husband encountered in inspiring enthusiasm for education in 1943, when they first came to Coco Hill:

> It was difficult at first because the people were superstitious. They didn't cooperate. They said that children couldn't achieve anything because of a belief that there was a pot of ram goat's blood buried in the crossroad and the children walked over it in coming to school. That prevented them from succeeding and doing well. They thought that if children walked over the pot, they wouldn't pass exams. They feared that if their child did well, a person would do evil to them. Teacher tried to remove these beliefs and children started to study for higher education and they passed exams. Little by little the fears were dispelled and a higher level of education was achieved.

In the past, parents frequently kept their children home from classes to work in the fields, to go to market, or to do household chores, and didn't encourage them to study for exams. Because secondary education was, in effect, unavailable to them, most rural villagers pinned their hopes for mobility on learning a trade, in the case of men, or becoming a seamstress, in the case of women. Since attending sewing school or becoming a tradesman's apprentice required a certain amount of cash and "connections," usually only children of more prosperous farmers followed this path. Small farmers and wage laborers in the community frequently told me that they had wanted to learn a trade or go to sewing school when younger but that their parents could not afford the expense.

Even after many had received this training, the limited market for their skills forced most to take up farming, at least on a part-time basis. The case of Thomas Porter, a 41-year-old black man, illustrates this pattern. In 1948, when he was 21, Mr. Porter went to Kingston to live with his uncle, a painter, who had agreed to teach him his trade. Mr. Porter learned how to paint in a few weeks and assisted his uncle in the latter's small business. His uncle did not have a lucrative trade, so Mr. Porter was forced to take up other jobs, such as gardening, to pay for room and board. After a year he moved out of his uncle's home into rooms of his own. He would find work occasionally as a painter but more often than not did no work at all. When his grandfather died in 1950 and left him four acres of land, he was only too ready to leave the city and return to Coco Hill. Once back in Coco Hill he tried to establish himself as a painter. However, there was little work available. During the year that I was in the community, he did one paint job for some friends on Percy Road and spent most of his time cultivating the land which he had inherited. He lives in the old three-room family house with his wife, who is a higgler, and their seven children. Mr. Porter is anxious for his children to be better educated than he is so that they will not have to follow in his footsteps; his eldest daughter attends JSC classes.

Most people in Coco Hill were not able to learn a trade at all, and had to seek other ways of getting cash. Some went to work as agricultural laborers, either in Jamaica or "in foreign"; others went to Kingston to find employment on the docks or in construction. Many were eventually drawn back to Coco Hill. Their hopes for significantly altering their life styles were frustrated by following unskilled occupations. They also missed their families, who could be relied on for emotional and financial support. An added incentive, for Mr. Porter and many others, was inheritance of land and houses in Coco Hill.

Similarly, many women who could not afford sewing school left Coco Hill to work as domestics. They returned to Coco Hill when they became pregnant, which almost inevitably occurred after a few years. Mrs. Pratt, a 35-year-old black woman, told me about her experiences:

> When I was fourteen mommy took me to a woman in Clarendon. Mommy grew with her. She kept a bake shop and made me work there. Have to look wood, chop wood, and carry it miles. I went there to learn sewing; she had two daughters who were seamstress but she never teach me at all. I was suffering. After a time, me just start to get disobedient. I was there a year and a month and she made me bake because it was compulsory. It wasn't on my mind so I don't digest it. I wasn't interested. I came home back. I go and do a little domestic work. Went first time to a policeman's wife. She paid me 5/– a week and the work was very hard. I was so little—I was sixteen but I was little in body. The house was seven apartment [rooms] and I have to scrub the floor and wash the clothes for seven children and herself and her husband and I have to cook and take the husband dinner to the station. I stayed there about three months. Came home back and was at home for a length of time. Then did domestic. Went to a town up Alexandria place. You have to take what you get. Get 6/– a week. Then I went to Trelawney. Was working 7/– a week. That was tip-top wages. Sometime when I remember those days . . . . There was quite nice, working with very nice people. When I was in Trelawney I got pregnant [by the man who worked in the yard for the same family]. Come home and that time was hard. When pregnancy three months got a job in Kingston and worked there 'til pregnancy eight months and one week. When I came out I still worked, doing a day work, washing and ironing. Then I have the baby and I stay at home with mommy.

Some villagers—usually wage laborers—continue to think in terms of traditional means of mobility, that is, learning a trade or taking up sewing. In addition, many still keep their children at home and do not send them to school regularly. However, the vast majority consider education the way to get ahead. Now that the hope of attending secondary school and training college has become more realistic for children in the village, parents are beginning to feel that education "counts" and to make the sacrifices necessary to send their children on.

The dramatic changes underlying these new attitudes are evident when one realizes that Coco Hill did not have even a primary school building until 1954. Prior to this time, classes were held in some of the local churches, a legacy from the days when education was the burden of the religious groups on the island. The first school was opened in the Methodist Church in the early 1880's. A few years later the Church of England (now the Anglican Church) was built and it, too, sponsored a school. According to individuals who attended these in the early part of the century, enrollment at each was about 150, although attendance was considerably lower. The two schools were consolidated in 1921 in response to a government regulation which directed certain existing denominational schools to join together and banned the subsequent opening of new denominational schools. Although the government then began to build public elementary schools, only a few areas benefited from this program, and Coco Hill was not one of them. The school met at the Anglican Church annex from 1921 to 1949. After 1949, when this church could no longer accommodate all of the children, the Burial Scheme Hall and the Tabernacle Baptist Church were also used as school rooms.

The primary school was built by the government after agitation by the Head Teacher and other concerned individuals in the community.* The school is still far from ideal. It consists of three long buildings set on a hill and the classrooms are separated only by blackboards. However, it represents a distinct improvement over the Anglican Church annex which was dark and overcrowded. A new infant center was completed in 1969 after the project was initiated by the now-defunct branch of the Jamaica Federation of Women in the mid-1950's. The infant center, which caters to children under six, was the focus of a bitter dispute over control of its land title between the Head Teacher and certain women in the Federation. The dispute

---

* Although the role of leaders in mobilizing public opinion in the community and making demands known to important government officials cannot be overlooked, it is also true that other factors are important. Politicians have always been anxious to win votes in Coco Hill and the success of particular demands is closely bound to party politics. In this particular case, although the Head Teacher was a Labourite (JLP), he made the demand on the behalf of a largely PNP constituency to a PNP Member of Parliament who was anxious to cement his support in Coco Hill.

paralyzed construction of the center for a number of years. The school is complete now, and is under the aegis of the Parent-Teacher Association. It is a government-aided enterprise which charges pupils 1/– a week in fees. These and a monthly government grant of £20 cover the salaries of the two untrained local teachers.

School enrollment has increased steadily since the 1940's, partly because of an awakened interest in education but also because there are now more school-aged children in Coco Hill. In 1943 enrollment at the school was 210 with a staff of five; in 1968 the enrollment had risen to 960 with 14 teachers and three interns. The infant school has 200 students.

Besides regular classes there are special sessions held at the school to prepare students for the Common Entrance Exam which they must pass to enter secondary school. There are also after-school classes to help students prepare for the Jamaica School Certificate Examination. Taking the JSC is second-best to attending high school. Those who attend the afternoon sessions at the Anglican Church annex are the boys and girls who have not been able to pass high school entrance exams and are hoping to accumulate enough passes to continue their training elsewhere or to qualify for certain jobs. Several women in their early 20's also attend the classes; they are young mothers who are anxious to get salaried employment so that they can, in turn, educate their children and have the extra cash to alter their life style.

A number of the children in Coco Hill attend high school in one of the nearby towns. Although a small number have always been able to advance by passing the Jamaica Local Examinations, no child from Coco Hill went to high school until 1953. By 1955 three had attended high school, by 1962 25 had attended high school, and by 1968 an estimated 70 were attending, or had attended, high school in the past five years; nearly all had won partial or full scholarships.

In the past, the villagers of Coco Hill viewed secondary schools as the private preserves of the light-skinned "up classes," institutions from which children of black rural farmers were excluded. A colored Jamaican gives a good description of the exclusive nature of the girls' school she attended:

> The life of the school, especially for the boarders, was cut off from the town, and indeed from everything around it—from the social and cultural mixture of Jamaican life and from communications with the outside world. We did not read the papers unless we were in the top forms . . . . We did not speak to the maids; we did not ask the day-girls to bring or buy anything for us . . . . Every Sunday . . . we filed into church, sat in a block by ourselves, and filed out afterwards without a word to our fellow

churchgoers. Occasionally we were taken to a film at the local
cinema . . . but on one occasion there was an epidemic in the
town; the head and staff of the school hesitated about exposing
the girls to infection in a shared cinema. The cinema was fumi-
gated, the school sat . . . in exclusive possession of the building,
and thereafter it was always arranged we had the cinema to our-
selves when we saw a film.[1]

This is a description of a secondary school located in a town only
nine miles from Coco Hill. People in the community were aware of the
exclusive nature of the school and many villagers mentioned that in
the past, no black girl could attend. The author of the quotation went
there in the mid-1940's when it was one of the most prestigious high
schools on the island. Today, six girls from Coco Hill—all black and
three from small farming families—are enrolled there on government
scholarships.[*]

Increased educational opportunities thus represent a significant
advance to the villagers. Nearly all in the village feel that if their
children study and have the "brain," then they can do well on examinations, attend secondary school, and qualify for good jobs. They frequently contrast their own deprivations with the opportunities available today for their children. For example, a poor elderly black woman
who does sewing part-time explained:

They have more improvement in education and everything. Because in my day we never have scholarship and all those thing
to help the children. You can get the money to loan from the
government and in our days we couldn't get any. There wasn't
so much improvement. I would say is better now. In our days
it was darker. Parents would never send their children to school
but now everyone rush to send their children to school. Those
were the darker days. We never have an infant school. If you feel
to go in our days, you go. Nobody rush you. A few of the older
people were educated but the rest, just stay home and do farming.

Another woman, a "stranger" who lives in a run-down shack, works
as a washer woman four days a week to support her five children, and
considers herself the poorest in her immediate neighborhood said:

You see, I had was to work when I was much younger and they
has not. We the parents work for them. They go to school more.
When I go to school I go barefoot and wear a dress for two weeks.

[*] The school is no longer considered the "elite institution" it once was. In
fact, it is common to hear white mothers and fathers of upper-class families in the
parish go on at great length about how standards of the school have deteriorated
and that they would never send their children to such a "common" school.

Today they must wear shoes and change dress two times a week. When I was in school, the thing was this. The teacher was interested but we never had as much privileges as these children. After you reach the sixth standard you just have to leave school. When I was a child like them we couldn't go to school so often and we never have the privilege to go to the different high school. The St. Hilary's school, no black children could go there. After we catch 14 or 15 the teacher tell us our time is up and we have to take the books and slate and return home. Today they can take the JSC.

Another woman, explaining to me why she would never want her children to do cultivating like herself, emphatically stated:

I would like my children to have a profession so they can get good money. You have to have the education now you know. Children take book now, man! Education! Education come first!

Finally, a woman who sends one son to high school compared her own situation to that of children today:

When I leave school, I was about 13. I was at home for a little time. I was interested in learning sewing but they couldn't realize it would be something great in the end. The first to commence were dark days. In my parents' days things weren't so. Even education wasn't so prevalent and today with people fussin' to get their children educated. Everybody in Coco Hill these days that have children trying with them. In my days parents wasn't so interested. I didn't go very often neither because I had to work. Come pimento time, I had to work, call Pimento Walk and they hire you. We were so poor that they would be able to buy a dress for the money I made in a week—they call it a "cover-me-naked," a cheap little thing. Our days in Jamaica was very rough for those who are poor. Sometimes maybe for three months drop into school one day or two. If I get the chance of going more often maybe I would do a little better. That's why I have to work so hard for my children. I would never like my children to have it hard like me.

The greater opportunity for rural children to attend secondary school has, paradoxically, reduced the worth of such an achievement from an island-wide perspective. For example, white-collar workers in Coco Hill would be disappointed if their children entered occupations similar to those they follow. Instead, they want their children to attend private preparatory schools, prestigious high schools in Kingston, and university, and to enter professions such as engineering, architecture, and the law.

Most people in Coco Hill have not yet begun to feel the impact of the decreased occupational currency of a secondary school diploma. However, their children may find when they graduate from high school that they are unable to enter the ranks of the island's elite until they have graduated from university. They may become disillusioned with the worth of what was considered a major achievement only a few years ago. They may also find that employment opportunities are extremely limited since educational developments have been outpacing changes in the society's occupational structure. However, to the majority in Coco Hill, it still means a great deal to go to secondary school and qualify for a low-level civil service or professional position. Most villagers tend to think of social mobility in terms of the traditional channels utilized by those in their own generation who became white-collar workers. They want their children to go to high school, to pass the JSC exams, or to enter training colleges. They also feel that if their children fail to qualify for secondary school or pass the JSC exams they can migrate to Kingston, or go abroad, and save the money they earn in low-status jobs to finance later training for more respected occupations.

CHILD-CENTEREDNESS

The position that the villagers occupy in the island-wide stratification system, their awareness of this position, the role of education in allocation to valued occupational roles, the stress on education by new political elites, and the increased availability of secondary education explain why the villagers place a high value on education. However, these factors do not explain the villagers' stress on their children's, rather than their own, opportunities for mobility.

A partial explanation is that an individual's prestige in the local status system is related to his children's educational attainments. Mr. Winston, for example, a big farmer and leader in many associations, was described to me by several villagers not in those terms, but as the father of two university-educated children. Similarly, many other men and women were deemed intelligent and worthy of esteem on the basis of their ability to send their children to secondary school and beyond.

One reason frequently given by the villagers to explain why they wanted to educate their children was that with education the children would be able to secure well-paid jobs and send money to them. A small farmer told me that he wanted his daughter to become a nurse and his son a policeman "because in that way, if their brain can take it, they could back themselves up and even help the mother and father too." Another woman, one who does some cultivating and is married to an employee at the lime factory, was about to have a hysterectomy. She was very depressed since she would not be able to have any more children. She had only two boys—one who attended high school. She told me:

> now that education get so popular, the children allow the parents to come up and be independent. Some people even have a little low hut and will just concrete the bottom and some of them will have 10 children and school them. After they get out, one or two would go to Kingston as a domestic and go to night school to advance himself, some go to England and America and let their parents independent. Parents don't want to give away their children today. They are so proud of their children now, so very much proud. In a few years I will be miserable. The young one is eight. I will be alone. . . . The children of today is the Minister of tomorrow. That child, in a few years, could be the Prime Minister.

The feeling that educating one's children is a kind of old-age insurance is not entirely grounded in fact. Although there are some cases where upwardly mobile children help their parents, it is these few which support the expectations of other struggling parents. For example, when the home of a man well respected in Coco Hill burned down, his children—two are policemen and one a clerk of court—came to the village the next day, and gave their parents money for new clothes, and lent them enough to begin rebuilding the house. Many parents boast new dresses and hats sent by their children from the United States or England, and display household ornaments given them by prosperous offspring. Several Coco Hill young people—primarily the unmarried—who have entered well-paid professions help finance the education of their younger siblings; other former Coco Hill residents, who have left children of their own behind, send occasional contributions toward their food, clothing, and school fees.

More frequently, those who "get on" relinquish their obligations to their parents, while those who stay in Coco Hill in low-status occupations usually contribute more faithfully, both in emotional and financial terms. For instance, a Coco Hill tailor sent his children to good secondary schools in Kingston; now most of them have migrated to England and America, and he complains that they never write to him. Even his daughter who is headmistress at a nearby primary school visits her father very rarely, and contributes only minimally to his support. The one son who has remained in Coco Hill—as a small farmer—sees his father every day, occasionally helps him in his work, and sends his children to the old man's house every evening with food. Similarly, one of the bigger farmers in Coco Hill, who is active in many associations, sent two of his children to university, sends his youngest to secondary school, and has two others who teach in schools in neighboring villages. None of the children sends money home. The two teachers, who live 25 miles away, visit Coco Hill once a year. Although the father indicated that his children's education is a great source of pride to him, on the few occasions when he sees them he feels uncomfortable and embarrassed. When one of his daughters, who goes to university in the United States, came back to Jamaica to renew her visa, she spent two days in Coco Hill. Her father lamented afterwards that she will probably marry a doctor or lawyer and be ashamed to introduce her parents to her husband.

This tendency for children to isolate themselves from the needs of their less mobile parents and other relatives is brought out most clearly in the cases of several white-collar "strangers" in the community. One teacher, whose husband is a bauxite company clerk, said that she rarely goes home to see her relatives, not only because the trip itself is expensive, but because she is expected to distribute gifts when she arrives. "You gone so long, and they look in your hand for five shillings to drop." Although both she and her husband earn fairly good salaries, she is hard put to make ends meet. She strives to maintain a respectable life style and to send each of her seven children to secondary school and possibly to university. She cannot afford to do this while distributing gifts of money to her relatives. Another teacher said that in some ways she was glad her parents were no longer living. If she had had to support them, she would never have been able to send her daughter to a private preparatory school or buy the nice house she lives in.

Meeting family responsibilities drains the resources of upwardly mobile persons who need every newly earned penny to consolidate their recently acquired status. A person in a white-collar job in rural Jamaica cannot afford to buy a new home, maintain a car, and educate his children on the salary he receives if he is also to contribute to the education of his siblings or send regular payments to his parents. The informal pressures to be unselfish and giving will be strong if he lives in the same community as the expectant relative. This is a basic reason for the exodus of upwardly mobile persons from their birthplaces. Another reason for leaving is to escape identification with low-status kin. An individual who becomes a white-collar worker will have a hard time establishing his new social worth among people who have known him all his life. His kin and neighbors will not treat him as a white-collar worker; in order to establish his new position and claim deference from relatives and friends, he will have to emphasize his newly superior status, and in doing so will almost inevitably antagonize his former peers. To establish his new status with a minimum of conflict, it becomes necessary for him to leave his home and go to a place where his origins are not visible.

Those who remain in Coco Hill as housewives and small farmers tend to give their parents more support, both emotionally and financially, than those who have gone away. They often provide their parents with meals, a place to sleep, and even cash—generosity which younger villagers often complain about, particularly when the beneficiary is an in-law. Nearly every elderly man or woman in Coco Hill lives close to at least one son or daughter and many had moved from one section of the community to another to achieve this closeness. They usually visit their child at least once a day, eat with him, and do favors for him in return. In the case of mothers and daughters, the two generations provide each other with a great deal of emotional support. The few elderly persons who have no children left in Coco Hill are extremely lonely. Although they often care for grandchildren or adopted children, they miss having children nearby to whom they feel close emotional bonds. Even if reluctant, children continue to feed and house their elderly parents, because there are many strong informal pressures on them to do so. If a son or daughter renounces his obligations and refuses to care for his father or mother, the wrath of his many relatives is hurled against him. He also runs the risk of losing part of his inheritance, something those who remain in Coco Hill and who have few financial resources cannot afford.

Most important in the villagers' desire to educate their children is the fact that they have transferred their own unfulfilled aspirations for mobility to their children. This is not a phenomenon unique to Jamaica; it is found in other stratified societies which emphasize egalitarian values but are structured so that success cannot be achieved by all. Such societies "presumably expose 'failures' to greater problems of adjustment to their station in life than do societies which accept as right or as normal the assumption that most people will remain in the station in which they were born; clearly, cultures which emphasize success require that individuals be able to adjust to personal failure." [2] One mechanism which resolves this contradiction is the "high degree of child-centeredness that encourages parents to seek satisfaction in high aspirations for their children when their own personal goals have not been achieved." [3]

From an island-wide perspective, adults in Coco Hill are already firmly established in specific status positions. They may move up in the local status hierarchy by expanding their land holdings or by purchasing modern appliances and new furniture, but this move is insignificant in relation to their rank in the national society; they are still defined as lower class. They cannot, at this stage in life, acquire the skills which would qualify them for prestigious and well-paid occupations and which would alter their status in the island-wide stratification system. The situation for their children is different. The latter have a "fresh start" from which they can move into high ranking positions. They can receive secondary education, qualify for professional and civil service occupations, and learn "proper" manners and speech patterns, whose significance depends on the other acquired attributes of respectability.

Limited employment and educational opportunities in Jamaican society mean, as they always have, that most rural villagers will fail to realize their status aspirations. Instead, they will be forced to take up farming and to follow a life style which is not dissimilar to that of their parents. By the time they reach middle age, both men and women in the community have relinquished hopes for their own mobility. They then project their own ambitions on to hopes for their children's success. As M.G. Smith notes in a study of occupational choice in rural Jamaica, "The measure of the adults' disappointment with their own lives is their aspiration on behalf of their children." [4] Thus, when adults in Coco Hill speak of emigrating to the United States or Canada, they say that it is to make enough money to educate their children.

Mobility aspirations for one's children deflect dissatisfactions and disappointments that might otherwise be expressed in forms which threaten the stability of the social order. Such aspirations are, in this sense, a source of stability in the society. However, there are other ways in which these frustrations are expressed—religious activity, acts of violence, drinking, sex, personal disputes, and obeah accusations.[*]

This is not to argue that the villagers are unaware of the inequities that exist in Jamaica or that "safety valves" drain off all hostilities against more successful members of the society. The villagers are very conscious of the contradictions between the egalitarian values proclaimed by politicians and other members of the elite and the realities of the island's class structure. They feel that they are not given an equal chance for achieving success, that the "haves" monopolize opportunities and advantages. They are acutely aware that persons of higher status look down upon them because they are poor, black farmers, but they feel that perhaps their children will not have to remain in this lowly position. This hope has been nourished in the past few years by the expansion of educational and employment oppor-

[*] The police records of Coco Hill reveal that from July 1965 to May 1969 there were 51 cases involving woundings and 91 involving assault, one involving assault with the intent to murder, one rape, and three assaults on the police.

tunities. But those at the bottom of the local status hierarchy, usually wage laborers and unsuccessful farmers, to whom the chances of educating their children still seem most remote,* do not entirely share this optimism.

* See Chapter V.

V

Correlates of
Educational Attainment

Although the residents of Coco Hill express enthusiasm for the new educational opportunities offered by the government, and there has been a steady increase since the early 1950's in the number of village children who go beyond primary school, only a relatively small percentage of children in the community enter post-primary institutions even now. What are the distinguishing characteristics of those families that send one or more children to post-primary school?

In considering this question, I draw on data gathered during a census of 101 households on Percy Road. In 56 of the households, there were children old enough to attend post-primary school or to have attended in the past five years; it is these households I will discuss. Since more white-collar workers live on Percy Road than in several other sections of Coco Hill, the number of children who attended post-primary institutions is somewhat higher than in the other sections. In the past five years, 27 children from Percy Road attended secondary school, seven attended university, one a home-craft center, one a police training school, one a telegraph school, and 10 attended JSC class.*

* Although JSC classes are held in a local church and are not part of a formal post-primary institution, these 10 were past school age, attended classes every day,

OCCUPATION AND LAND OWNERSHIP

Of those on Percy Road who have sent one child or more to post-primary institutions in the past five years, six were white-collar workers, 19 were small, independent farmers, three were big farmers or enterpreneurs, and one was a wage laborer. In addition to cultivating, the farmers usually pursue another cash-yielding occupation, and often hire labor. The only man in this group who works out as an agricultural laborer is a penner, or cattle tender, for a white property owner in the district. His son attends the JSC classes, but is a butt of ridicule among the teachers, who find it amusing and somewhat sad that he believes he can pass the exams, since he can barely read or write. He and his parents are anxious for him to "get on" and he attends classes regularly and produces the few pounds necessary to take the exams. At present, he is one of only two boys in the village who willingly hires himself out to weed grass for better-off villagers, usually teachers. As he weeds the yards of white-collar workers, he withstands the taunts of his friends, who tell him that he is "fool fool" to do such menial work for such low wages.

As for the women in households which send one or more children to post-primary school, 83 per cent engage in cash-yielding activities; none are full-time cultivators and only three are full-time housekeepers. Most of the women do part-time cultivating and go to market to sell their own and their spouse's produce; many others engage in occupations such as teaching, clerical work, shopkeeping, and higglering. Of the four female-headed households with successful children, two are headed by unmarried teachers who are raising children of relatives, one is headed by a shopkeeper, and the fourth by a seamstress who is the widow of a successful farmer.

The occupations, land holdings, and income of persons in this group enable them to maintain a desired style of life. Many have modern furniture in their homes, and private catchment tanks; some have modern appliances. Except for the white-collar workers, who achieved their occupational status through education, most acquired land from their parents, learned a trade when younger, or, in the cases of five of the men, earned cash doing farm contract work in the United States during the 1940's.

Even though they are comparatively well off by Coco Hill stan-

did homework, and took a number of exams each year. Of the 10, six passed at least one subject, two qualified for post office jobs, and one received a promotion in the prison system on the basis of his exam results. It is generally only those who have done well in primary school who attend these classes.

dards, few have the large cash reserves needed to finance their children's education. Many had to sell land in order to pay school fees. One of the most successful farmers in the community, a man who owns about 30 acres of land, told me, "I could have much more cows but I have to be selling them for school fees." The wife of a successful small farmer explained how difficult it was to find cash for books and uniforms for her daughter, even though the girl had a partial scholarship to secondary school:

> At the school, them ask one week for the children to buy one of these binders. At that time it was cabbage time and cabbage was only selling for a penny a pound. So I went to market at four in the morning and I stayed all day. I managed to get 30/–. So I went to the store. The binder and the paper them cost 25/– and there was only 5/– to buy the groceries for the whole week. At that school them always asking the children to buy this and that and the binder just sit in the house and she never use it one earthly time. But we have to deprive ourself to help our children so they can get qualification to help them out. Else they have to be a common laborer. We must have some sort of ambition to carry on.

The cash in the household pays for the daughter's school expenses —her books, uniform, and bus fare total about £7 a month, a large sum in Coco Hill. Her husband, who worked in the United States on the farm contract when he was young, sold four acres of land to help meet school expenses.

Generally, those who do not send their children to post-primary school own little if any land and do not regularly pursue cash-yielding occupations other than farming. They earn cash by working as agricultural laborers.

For several reasons they do this type of work to earn enough to keep their families clothed and fed, and do not seek to accumulate large cash reserves in this way. One might expect that those whose own land does not yield sufficient income for their needs, and who have no supplementary occupation, would work to save enough money to buy more land, to purchase consumer items, and educate their children. There is no scarcity of agricultural jobs in Coco Hill—big farmers constantly complain that they cannot get men to work for them, and the *Daily Gleaner* frequently chronicles the difficulties that sugar estates have in finding laborers. However, agricultural work in Coco Hill is poorly paid and the demand is erratic, often coming when the individual needs to work on his own land. Further, working out in this capacity is considered demeaning; men in the village do not like to be seen working on someone else's land. It is felt to be degrading to subordinate oneself to another villager, who may be a neighbor, kinsman, or fellow church member and who, from the perspective of the national society, is also a "poor farmer." Raymond Smith writes, "in a society where status is determined not only by occupational or technical efficiency but also by colour, birth into a local or a kinship group, and cultural attainments, a potential employee is less likely to accept a subordinate role in relation to someone fairly close to him in the status scale than in relation to one who is more distant." [1]

For example, a middle-aged black landless laborer told me that he refused to work out for others because, "I wouldn't work with some of the people them. You quarrel with them, insult you, tell you had word, don't pay you. Prefer to work with Mr. McNeil [a colored property owner]. He treat them good. Is not the wages, is the way he handle them." Small farmers are considered bad risks, not only because they often do not have the cash on hand to pay their workers, but also because they may use the situation, or seem to do so, in order to emphasize their superior status. Men who must work out prefer to work for big property owners, where status distinctions are clear— the laborers occupy a position subordinate to the white or colored planter in all social relations. However, there are relatively few big farmers whose status is so clearly superior.

Many who hire out to other farmers in the district resolved the resulting inner conflict to themselves, and to me, by explaining that they work out for a particular man because they are friends. In some cases, the friendships are real, but in most instances the employer is of higher status than the employee and the relationship between them is not one of equality.

The big farmers as well as white-collar workers who wish to hire labor try to overcome the villagers' reluctance to work out by "courting" laborers. A number of big farmers told me that they had to treat their employees well so that they would continue to work for them. The big farmers invite them to eat at their homes and offer them drinks. When the employer is a white-collar worker, the laborers may acquire prestige among their peers by telling them of this favored treatment by high-status individuals. For example, Mr. Douglas, a white-collar worker, regularly hired a fellow church member to clear the bush for him. Mr. Douglas was careful to treat the man well, to pay him good wages, and to extend favors to him. He also used to sit with him, drinking and talking, for hours after the work was finished. The relationship, however, was clearly an unequal one, symbolized by the terms of address used: the worker called Mr. Douglas "Mass John," * but Mr. Douglas

* It is a symbol of respect to call a man "Mass."

called the worker Mr. Harding. Mr. Harding did not enter his employer's home from the front, as white-collar friends did, and he ate his meals alone on the back verandah rather than with the Douglas family. He told me, however, that he would work only for Mass John because the latter treated him very well and was his good friend.

Men explain their disinclination to work as cane cutters on sugar estates—a situation in which there is no problem of near-equality with one's employer—by saying that the distance from home is too great, but there are clearly other factors involved; the nearest sugar estate is only five miles from Coco Hill. Cane cutting is hard, seasonal work, and the pay is low. It is traditionally a low-status job, associated with slavery and low rank. When I asked informants if members of their family had ever cut cane at the nearby estate, many answered that no one in their family had ever had to do such a thing. The reluctance to cut cane has increased over the years as alternate means of wage employment have become available in the bauxite industry, light manufacturing, and tourism. A man who needs extra cash tries to get a job on a construction crew at a hotel site, in the mines of the bauxite companies, or even in one of the local factories before he considers going to cut cane at a sugar estate.

The majority of women in households where children do not go beyond primary school do not pursue any cash-yielding occupation. Most are full-time housekeepers and several help their spouses in farming. Those who do earn cash usually work out on an irregular basis in low-status and low-paid jobs such as washing or domestic work. Like their male counterparts who try to avoid working out as agricultural laborers or cane cutters, they prefer not to do domestic work or washing for better-off women in the community. In female-headed households with unsuccessful children, the woman—often a spinster or widow—usually engages in full-time cultivation of less than an acre of land. A daughter and grandchildren by different children may live with her. In some cases, the daughter engages in occasional labor, usually as a domestic. In general, female-headed households are among the poorest in the village.

EDUCATION

Parents who send their children to post-primary school have not attained a higher level of education than those whose children do not go on. Except for white-collar workers, most adults in the community attended school until the sixth grade—the highest primary grade. This does not reflect the actual amount of time spent in school, since many who were formally enrolled only "dropped in" a day or two of the entire month.

MARITAL STATUS

There is no significant difference in marriage rates between those who do and do not send children to post-primary school. In all but one male-headed household which sent one or more children to post-primary school in the past five years, the man is married. Similarly, only four couples who do not send children to post-primary school are still living in common-law unions. In these cases, the men are under the age of 40 and only one child in the household is old enough to have attended a post-primary school; the rest still attend primary school. It is highly probable that they will get married in the next few years, following a pattern that is typical for most farmers in Coco Hill.

Marriage occurs relatively late in rural Jamaica—usually when the couple are in their early or middle 30's. Most men and women have a number of affairs in their late teens or early 20's, but these do not usually involve common residence. Instead, young men and women remain attached to their parents' households; the women help with household chores and the men help in the fields, work for cash (often outside the community), and contribute money to the maintenance of the household. As the men grow older, they find that to maintain their economic and social freedom, they must break away and set up their own homes. To do this requires a mate, since a man will want someone to care for the house, to wash and cook, and to take his crops to the local market. He generally rents rooms in the community and takes up residence with the mother of his most recent children. When he has achieved a minimal level of economic security, that is, accumulated enough money to buy his own home and some land, or inherited a home and land from his parents, he usually gets married.*

Even if the man does not achieve this level of economic security, there are pressures which induce him to marry. William Davenport, in a detailed study of family patterns in rural Jamaica, effectively argues that if a man has little security and then, through a series of nonlegal unions, assumes responsibility for several illegitimate children, in addition to his obligations to parents and grandparents, the resulting

---

* When a man and woman do get married, they often bring some of their illegitimate children by other partners into the newly established household. As far as I could tell, illegitimacy or legitimacy did not appear to affect educational aspirations for children; several successful high school students in Coco Hill were illegitimate children. Most of them had been raised by their mothers.

conflict of loyalties makes his position very difficult. "The more frequent alternative is for a man to move toward a consolidation of all his obligations and potential assets by setting up a household around a permanent marriage. With meagre resources, this is extremely difficult, but it is the only way in which he can fulfill all his obligations of kinship, and at the same time lay the groundwork for security in his own declining years and return to dependency." [2] Thus, Davenport points out that marriage is not an index of social mobility. Rather, it is an integral part of the life cycle which domestic groups in rural communities experience.

FAMILY ENVIRONMENT AND THE STRUCTURE OF COCO HILL SCHOOL

Another factor related to success in sending children to post-primary school is the environment provided in the household. Parents who send their children to post-primary school are not only able to provide more nourishing food than those who do not, but make particular efforts to further their children's success. For example, they try to give their children special places to study, which is easier to do in a two- or three-room house than in a one-room shack. They encourage their children to spend time doing homework and often release those studying for exams from household duties. Parents save money to clothe their children well, buy books for school, and pay school and examination fees. They put tremendous pressure on their children to do well, chastising them for failing to work hard or if they do poorly on exams. They continually emphasize the need to excel in class in order to win government scholarships and gain entry to secondary school.

Children of white-collar workers, particularly teachers, have further advantages; their parents can help them with school work, and books, newspapers, and magazines are often available in their homes. Since white-collar workers are usually friendly with teachers at the primary schools, the latter often pay special attention to their children in class.* In addition, several teachers tutor their own children after school and during the summer holidays. They obtain special books designed to prepare students for the Common Entrance Examination and require their children to spend many hours during the holidays practicing the exercises.

---

* White-collar workers who send their children to private preparatory schools usually place the children in public primary schools for the year in which they take the Common Entrance Examination. Since the government awards more scholarships to children from public schools, their children have a good chance of winning them.

Parents who do not send their children to post-primary school often cannot, because of their limited economic resources, provide their children with an environment conducive to academic success. Their children are usually poorly clothed and fed, and often suffer from worm infections. They sleep in one room shacks with as many as 10 to 12 other persons; their parents frequently keep them home from classes to help in the fields or with household chores.

Furthermore, the structure of the school in Coco Hill does not give the children of wage laborers and unsuccessful small farmers an equal chance for achievement. Classes in the school are very large, usually over 100—for example, the class in which children learn to read has an enrollment of 250 and only one teacher. The teacher usually seats the children of more respected members of the community, whom she knows and wants to help, on the front benches. The rest sit towards the back and often cannot even hear what the teacher is saying or get her attention. Most teachers tend to concentrate on the brightest children in their classes and give up hope that they can help the rest; under these classroom circumstances, the brightest children appear to be those whom she has favored to begin with.

CHURCH AFFILIATION

There are eight churches in Coco Hill: the Tabernacle Baptist Church has 167 members, the Seventh Day Adventist Church 143, the Church of God 117, the Pentecostal Church 115, the Roman Catholic Church 61, the Methodist Church 58, the Baptist Church 57, and the Anglican Church 54. Those who send their children to post-primary school affiliate with one of the local churches and are more often regular churchgoers than those whose children do not attend post-primary institutions.

Church membership is closely correlated with rank in the local status hierarchy. White-collar workers, big farmers and entrepreneurs, and successful small farmers tend to join those churches associated with the Jamaican elite—the Anglican, Roman Catholic, Methodist, and Baptist Churches. Affiliation with these churches is a symbol of prestige, and members, particularly white-collar workers, boast that their denominations' services are "dignified" and "cultured."

The majority of the members of the Tabernacle Baptist * and

* The Tabernacle Church in the parish of St. Ann dates from the 1876 split in the Baptist Church. Dr. Johnston, a Scottish missionary, founded the Tabernacle Church when he was accused of misrepresenting the work of the Baptist Church in letters to the English press. A commission of four missionaries met and threatened to expel him from the church. Johnston won over a significant sector of the Baptist constituency and founded his own church—the Evangelistic mission. He presided

Seventh Day Adventist Churches are small, independent farmers, although a few white-collar workers and a number of big farmers and entrepreneurs also belong. Persons in the higher-status groups, however, tend to serve as church officials rather than as ordinary members. Both churches impose certain restrictions on their members, and services are more lively than in the most respected churches. Members clap their hands while they sing and respond to sermons with shouts of "Amen" and "Praise the Lord," and there are set periods in the sermons when the brethren can ask questions and make comments.

The Pentecostal Church and the Church of God—both founded within the past 15 years in Coco Hill—appeal to less successful small farmers and wage laborers. The distinguishing feature of these churches is the "born again" experience, that is, the fact that members receive communications from the Holy Ghost and go into trancelike states, when they "speak in tongues," or talk in strange languages while supposedly possessed by the Holy Ghost. Being "born again" or "saved" enables one to "lose the taste for things which aren't right, to live for the Lord and to love the Bible." The main object of the services is to evoke this experience and many "tarry for the Lord" after the meetings to try, by singing and praying, to be "saved." The churches are also marked by the practice of baptising members by total immersion, and by a high degree of emotional participation in the services. Members sing throughout the services, clap their hands, move their bodies, and at times are free to walk around the church. The brethren do not pray in silence but, at several points in the service, are told by the minister or elder, "Let us pray," at which time each says his own prayer aloud and extemporizes, pouring out his troubles and woes. Like the Baptist Tabernacle and Seventh Day Adventist Churches, they sponsor almost nightly activities and impose certain restrictions on members.

There is not only a close correlation between church membership and the educational success of children, but many of the parents of successful children affiliate with specific churches. Nearly 70 per cent of the parents of successful children (and 85 per cent of the farmers, primarily small farmers, in this category) are affiliated with either the Baptist Tabernacle, Seventh Day Adventist, Pentecostal Churches, or Church of God. The doctrines these churches espouse and their concomitant behavioral restrictions provide ethical encouragement for individuals to work hard and save in order to "get on" in the world.

In the Pentecostal Church and the Church of God, the central

over the nine branches of the church, was a physician, and represented the parish in the island's Legislative Council for many years. Today the Baptist Church and the Tabernacle Church exist in harmony and there are only very subtle differences between them in doctrine and ritual.

doctrine is salvation through the personal acceptance of God. Once a person is "saved," he then has the strength to live a "godly" and "Christian" life. Although the Baptist Tabernacle and Seventh Day Adventist Churches do not follow this doctrine, they, too, emphasize ascetic values and the fact that members, as "true Christians," must refrain from worldly pleasures such as drinking, gambling, smoking, and dancing. Members must also work hard at their occupations. In all four churches the brethren are urged to educate their children and are told not to be daunted by disappointments and failures, or by the envy of kin and neighbors.

The religious beliefs of these churches strengthen their members' commitment to mobility. The "godly" or the "saved" do not spend money frivolously on entertainment, nor, as one woman told me, do they merely "sit in the shop and loaf and make big noise." Instead, they conscientiously strive to "get on" by working hard and saving their money.

These churches reinforce the motivations of their members to strive for their own, or, more likely, their children's mobility. For example, only by thrift and hard work can they afford to finance private lessons for their children and to pay for JSC classes and examination fees; this is in contrast to white-collar workers whose regular and relatively high salaries provide the economic resources necessary to finance not only their children's education but their leisure time activities and entertainment as well. The determination of "saved" individuals—especially women—to encourage their children's success may also affect the children's educational achievement in other ways. Since such people lead a "godly" life and are hard workers, they tend to be respected by teachers, who are then interested in helping their children in school. This is particularly important for small farmers, whose children would not ordinarily receive special attention from teachers.

The fact that these villagers are "true Christians" and follow the dicta of the churches legitimizes their success to some extent. Those who have achieved desired goals are often perceived as selfish or proud by less successful villagers of similar status. I discuss in Chapter VI how this envy often leads to disputes; however, the fact that a successful person is a "true Christian" and follows the path of righteousness justifies his achievements to those of lower status as well as to himself.

Conversely, those who do not send their children to post-primary school are less likely to be church members or even churchgoers. Thus, 33 per cent of the parents of unsuccessful children are unaffiliated with any church; nearly 70 per cent of these are male. (In nearly every church, women outnumber men. In the Pentecostal Church and the

Church of God this is especially marked; women make up over 75 per cent of the congregations. The high rate of attendance for women is linked to several factors: the cathartic nature of the church services, the informal taboos on women's participation in other types of activities which afford emotional release such as drinking at rum shops, and the status-enhancing functions of church membership.) An exploration of why certain individuals refrain from churchgoing and church member-ship, even though belonging to church is a mark of prestige in the community, requires a detailed analysis of many complex and inter-related factors which are beyond the scope of this study. Here I merely suggest a few factors which may be operating.

Those who do not belong to church or attend regularly tend to be wage laborers and unsuccessful small farmers, that is, those at the bottom of the local status hierarchy. They refrain from participation in church activities in part because of their low economic status and the accompanying belief that there is little chance for altering their own or their children's status. These villagers say that they cannot go to church because they cannot afford to buy "proper" church clothes or to pay church dues. However, the same persons who give this excuse often spend large amounts of money on rum, cigarettes, and gambling.

If it is assumed that persons are most likely to defer immediate gratification of their needs and pleasures when they seem to have a reasonable chance of achieving their goals, the behavior of non-church-goers makes sense. Wage laborers and unsuccessful small farmers accept the status-defining criteria of the Jamaican stratification system; they would like their children to go to secondary school and enter desirable occupations. However, because of their perception of their own low status, they do not consider these goals realistic. Thus, those at the lowest levels of the local status system have already defined the situation as unpromising for their children; their life style, occupation, income, and social interactions reinforce this definition every day. They are therefore unwilling to save their money or adhere to the ascetic restrictions imposed by some churches. Instead, they spend their extra cash in ways such as drinking rum, which afford instant gratification and some measure of escape. They do not perceive that this behavior blocks their own or their children's chances for future success. Moreover, church values which encourage the brethren to work hard and to refrain from worldly pleasures have little appeal for persons to whom hard work means pursuing an unrewarding low-status occupation. In addition, the poorest villagers are frequently discouraged by better-off villagers—particularly their kin—from attending church activities and services. Villagers who have acquired higher status would be embarrassed by the presence of low-status relatives, for they are anxious to preserve their own status and to avoid identification with their unprestigious kin.

The fact that these persons are not church members or church-goers may have further negative consequences. In contrast to church members they have not internalized—at least not to the same extent—the values which church doctrines tend to emphasize regarding the need to make sacrifices in the struggle to secure advancement. Of course, one cannot know whether, even if the poorest villagers fully accepted the ascetic practices presumably necessary for upward mobility, many of them, or their children, would be successful.

SEX ROLE DIFFERENTIATION AND EDUCATION: A SPECIAL CASE

Approximately the same number of boys and girls from Coco Hill attend secondary school. However, of the 30 students who attended JSC classes when I lived in the village, only two were male. This pre-ponderance of girls in the JSC classes is typical not just of Coco Hill but of communities throughout the island; it is surprising when one considers that so many young men in the community have no jobs, refuse to work on the land, and express a desire to "get on." It might be supposed that one way to alter their occupational status would be to attend the classes, pass the exams, and continue their educational training. Their minimal representation at the JSC classes can be traced to several factors.

First, the occupations available to girls who wish to move up in the island status hierarchy in terms of earnings and prestige—such as teaching, nursing, and secretarial work—require secondary school training or success on the JSC exams. In contrast, boys have occupa-tional opportunities which do not require such training; the bauxite, tourist, and new light manufacturing industries, and the increased transportation services, offer a growing number of jobs for men with technical and mechanical skills. These jobs offer high salaries. To qualify for them a young man need not pass the JSC exams but must merely acquire specific mechanical or technical skills. This can be done through apprenticeship programs, technical schools, or special training programs offered by some of the companies.

However, one might still expect that some young men would aspire to occupations which require a certain number of passes on the JSC exams, clerical work or positions in the police force, for example. Although many young men indicated that they desired to qualify for such jobs, they were, at the same time, reluctant to attend the JSC classes. This reluctance stems from the different roles that men and women play in the household and the different occupational expectations which apply to them. It is perfectly acceptable for a girl to stay at home and to help her mother with household chores—in fact, she is expected to do this. She can attend the JSC classes while performing this role, spend part of every afternoon at school, and take some time out to study for the exams. She is not pressured to take all the exams in one year and can enter training college a few years after finishing primary school.

This is not true for the young men in the community. A man's role is not to do household chores. As one informant put it, "A girl, they fit naturally into the home life. But the boy, he can fetch wood but that is only an hour." A man in Jamaica is supposed to provide for his family. Young men do not see how they can do this in the style that they desire by remaining small farmers. They consider all agricultural labor demeaning and rightly perceive that they will not be able to accumulate enough cash through small-scale farming to fulfill their increased consumption needs. Some have learned a trade, but cannot find steady jobs in these occupations. To stay in Coco Hill for several years studying for the JSC exams, while having nothing else to do except work in their parents' fields or work out for others in menial jobs, is repugnant to them. Instead, all expressed a desire to get a job off the land quickly so that they could begin to acquire the clothing, radios, televisions, cars, and other consumption items that they dream of, and establish their status as nonagricultural workers independent of their parents. Studying for the JSC exams is, to them, too long range and uncertain a project; instead, they prefer to try to get semiskilled jobs or migrate to "foreign." If, as often happens, these opportunities do not materialize, they may end up having nothing to do at all, a situation which changes for most young men only when they finally relinquish their dreams of success and get unskilled nonagricultural jobs or, more commonly, take up farming.

CONCLUSION

The findings reported in this chapter reveal that success in sending children to post-primary school is closely linked to economic status. Children of white-collar workers, big farmers and entrepreneurs, and successful small farmers stand a much better chance of qualifying for secondary school than those of wage laborers. Small farmers who are successful in sending their children to post-primary school usually engage in another cash-yielding occupation, as do their wives. They, or their wives, often affiliate with one of the churches in the community which emphasizes the need to work hard and to save and which imposes restrictions on the leisure activities of members which would otherwise drain off cash from the household. Thus, following a "Christian" or "godly" life promotes behavior and attitudes which facilitate educational advancement of children. But attending church appears to be linked, at least partially, to economic status: villagers who do not attend church tend to be those at the lowest level of the local status hierarchy.

Within the entire community, approximately one out of every seven children attends a post-primary institution.[*] Although this represents a significant advance to most villagers, it means that the majority still do not send their children to post-primary school. In fact, the frustrations and disappointments of those whose children do not attend post-primary school or pass the JSC exams are heightened precisely because more children in Coco Hill than ever before have been able to pursue their education past Coco Hill School. In the following chapter I show that rivalry between parents whose children qualify for secondary school or other post-primary education and those whose children are not successful students is a principal cause of disputes in the community. In the concluding chapter some of the broader societal implications of this blocked mobility are suggested.

[*] This estimate is based on (1) the number of children attending post-primary school in Coco Hill and (2) an estimate of the proportion of the population in the age group eligible to attend post-primary school in the whole village, extrapolated from a census of Percy Road.

VI

Disputes and
Educational Mobility

The system of formal education serves important integrative functions in Jamaican society. The schools inculcate certain civic values and "appropriate" models of behavior and, if successful,* induce members of the society to accept as legitimate society-wide criteria for success and the prescribed means for achieving success. In previous chapters I have shown that the villagers of Coco Hill aspire to emulate the life style of the island's elite, and those who do not fulfill their own mobility aspirations transfer them to their children. They believe that the best way to achieve success is through the increased educational opportunities available to them.

However, the data reveal that most children in the village do not qualify for post-primary schools; this leads to frustration and disappointment. Many who are unsuccessful feel that perhaps they can emigrate, save money, and eventually finance their own, or their children's schooling. In this chapter I suggest that one way in which these frustrations are expressed—serving as a safety valve and therefore a source of stability in the larger society—is quarreling with those

* In a society like Jamaica, in which political elites claim that they are equalizing access to mobility, this success depends primarily on the degree to which opportunities for mobility are available and are perceived as available.

in the local system who have been successful. Those who are not successful in educating their children do not question the value of education; they envy those whose children have passed exams or entered secondary and training schools.

Because secondary education has acquired an important symbolic significance in the local system of prestige ranking, sending one's children to secondary school may have important consequences for patterns of interaction in the village. Qualifying for secondary school is an indication of a child's future occupational success and can thereby enhance his parents' prestige. The child's success can arouse envy and jealousy in other villagers and become a source of disputes, or, as the villagers would say, "fuss." Before I elaborate on these points, it is helpful to consider two such disputes which occurred while I was in the community.

TWO SOCIAL SITUATIONS

"You Think We Are Fool and Can't Pass Exam"

The Huntleys are "strangers" to Coco Hill although they have been living in the community for over 12 years. They live on Percy Road in an old rented house with a living room, kitchen, and three bedrooms divided by curtains. They have a new refrigerator, a record player-radio set, and a fair-sized catchment tank which supplies their water needs. The head of the household is a dark-skinned man from a respected family in the principal town of another parish. He went to a prestigious secondary school, has worked in industry, and currently has a top post in the St. Ann Parish branch of a government agency. His annual salary is £1,500, very high by Jamaican standards. His brothers and sisters are all well-placed in the society; one is a doctor, another a high school teacher, and many of his nieces and nephews have been to prestigious secondary schools and to university.

Mrs. Huntley, a fair-skinned woman, comes from a rural community in the parish of St. James, where her family is highly respected. Her sisters and brothers are also in "good positions"; some are teachers, one attends university, and the others have white-collar jobs in Kingston. Mrs. Huntley, a teacher, works in a nearby town, mainly because she does not get along with the Head Teacher in Coco Hill. She feels that he has slighted her family and she claims that he has spread rumors that her son, now 17 and attending secondary school on a government scholarship, "wouldn't come to anything." This upset Mr. and Mrs. Huntley very much. Mrs. Huntley says that the Coco Hill school does not get good exam results, that one of the teachers drinks too much, and that the Head Teacher would not help her children do well in school. Although Mrs. Huntley no longer refuses to speak to the Head Teacher, she still feels that his disparaging remark about her son was insulting, especially since the children of teachers are traditionally treated well at school. She therefore refuses to teach in the community, although this would be more convenient for her, and takes all of her primary-aged children with her to the town school where she works. This is resented by the other teachers in Coco Hill who feel that she is acting "uppety." Although they secretly envy Mrs. Huntley for taking her children to a more solidly middle-class school than the one in Coco Hill, they say resentfully that Mrs. Huntley feels that Coco Hill School is not good enough for her children, and feel that her preference implies a slight to their own worth, since they send their own children to school in Coco Hill.

The Huntleys have seven children: one baby, four at primary school, and two at secondary school. They also have a full-time maid who does most of the household chores and cares for the baby while Mrs. Huntley works. The parents put tremendous pressure on their children to do well in school and to win scholarships, since they cannot afford to pay high school tuition for all of them. The eldest son hopes to enter the University of the West Indies to study economics, and the eldest daughter, who is first in her class at a prestigious girls' school, wants to be a librarian.

The Huntleys' neighbors across the road, the Gordons, live in rooms behind the large grocery store and attached rum shop that Mr. Gordon runs. Although the dwelling looks run-down from the outside, the family's furniture is modern and comfortable; in fact, the Gordons own a television set. The household includes four children, Mr. Gordon's mother, and a maid. All four of the children attend a private preparatory school in the town where Mrs. Huntley teaches. Mr. Gordon supplements his income from the shops by transporting bananas in an old truck from small farms in Coco Hill to the boxing plant. He also owns an acre of land which he rents to others in the district. Mr. Gordon, a black man, is a native of Coco Hill. He has one brother, who lives in St. Ann's Bay, the parish capital, and runs a trucking service. Mr. Gordon's wife, also black, comes from a large town in the parish of St. Ann; she tends the rum shop while her husband minds the grocery. Mr. Gordon is respected within the community, a man to whom people come with their problems as well as with requests for loans, transportation, and advice. Unfortunately, however, the Gordon children are not successful scholars, although they go to private school.

The following incident occurred while I was in Coco Hill, and was a popular topic of conversation for many days. This is Mrs. Huntley's version:

> Right now the Gordons aren't speaking to us. It happened since Louis [the Huntleys' eldest son] passed his exams in December. Dawn [the Huntleys' eldest daughter] went to church one Sunday and on the way home on the road she said to one of the Gordon children, "You must be better disciplined." They were making a lot of noise and fuss. After that they [the Gordons] stop speaking to us. Was one week after Louis passed his exams and their children call name at mine. One day I was telling my children not to pay them no mind and Mr. Gordon called, "You think we are fool and can't pass exam." So you see what is at the root of it. They are covetous, their children can't pass exam. They spread a rumor that they saw a man leaving Dawn's window one night. Their relatives don't speak to us either. And I don't send the children to travel to school with Mr. Gordon anymore.

Social relations between the two families have been strained for many years, mainly because the Gordons are sensitive to the Huntleys' claims to superior status. Mr. Huntley associates with some of the "big shots" in the parish, who frequently drive by and stop to visit. Mrs. Huntley is friendly with other white-collar workers in the area. In fact, her best friend is a woman who attended the University of the West Indies and now teaches at a teacher training college in the parish. The Huntleys came into the community as "strangers" of high status and have only one kinship tie in Coco Hill, Mrs. Huntley's second cousin, who is the wife of one of the most respected men in the village. Mr. and Mrs. Huntley are what Robert Merton calls "cosmopolitan influentials," that is, influential individuals who derive their prestige and influence, not from their social relations within the community, but from their previous achievements and previously acquired skills: "Typically a newcomer to the community, he [the cosmopolitan influential] does not and cannot utilize personal ties as his chief claim to attention. He usually comes into the town fully equipped with the prestige and skills associated with his business or profession and his 'worldly' experience. He begins the climb in the prestige-structure at a relatively high level." [1]

In contrast, Mr. Gordon fits into Merton's category of "local influential," a man whose "influence rests on an elaborate network of personal relationships . . . . He must overcome the obstacle of being intimately known to the community when he was 'just a kid.' He must somehow enable others to recognize his consistent change in status. Most importantly, people to whom he was once subordinate must be brought to the point of now recognizing him as, in some sense, superordinate." [2] Mr. Gordon comes from a respected family in the community—his father owned over 10 acres of land and was a tradesman and a leader at the Baptist Tabernacle Church—and he himself has been upwardly mobile. Following the traditional pattern of mobility in Coco Hill, Mr. Gordon and his brother learned a trade, and over the years, Mr. Gordon has managed to purchase the grocery shop, buy a truck, and set up a rum shop. He did not go beyond the sixth class in school and neither did his wife. In contrast to Mr. and Mrs. Huntley, who have achieved post-primary education themselves, the Gordon children are the first generation of their family to have the opportunity to attend secondary school and, therefore, to qualify for professional or civil service posts.

Within the community, Mr. Gordon has more influence than Mr. Huntley. He was frequently listed in the survey of respected persons in the community and villagers interact with him as subordinates. On the other hand, Mr. and Mrs. Huntley were never mentioned in the survey—neither works in Coco Hill or is active in local associations. They have been more successful in establishing equal social relations with prestigious persons outside the community, something which the Gordons have been unable to do, but they have also been the butt of much hostility from other white-collar workers in the village, whose esteem they wish to have. As I mentioned, many teachers resent Mrs. Huntley; they feel that she is haughty and proud, and that she flaunts her children's achievements, her husband's position in the government agency, and his educational background. Since they believe themselves to be the Huntleys' equals in status, the other teachers resent their assumptions of superiority. They do not, however, feel threatened by the Gordons, since Mr. Gordon lacks education and prestigious school ties and has no pretensions of superiority to teachers.

The Huntleys and Gordons do generally make an effort to maintain amicable relations with each other. This is not only because they are neighbors; it is also because the two families depend on each other for many favors and because, in the context of Coco Hill, both families recognize that they are of higher status than the majority. Thus, Mr. Huntley often chats with Mr. Gordon or drinks with him in the rum shop. The Gordon and Huntley children are good friends, since they are among the few who go to school outside Coco Hill. Mr. Gordon frequently drives Mrs. Huntley and her children to school, and has on several occasions driven members of the Huntley family to the doctor in a nearby town, free of charge. However, the Gordons do resent the Huntleys, and feel that the Huntleys boast of their achievements and do not accept their neighbors as equals. This resentment is evidenced in Mr. Gordon's statement, "You think we cannot pass exam." Moreover,

Mr. Gordon goes to Mr. Huntley for help in filling out his income tax forms, and this, too, puts him in a subordinate position, one that emphasizes his lack of education and resulting inferior status.

Given this background, it is understandable that the academic performance of the children in both families is a sensitive subject, particularly to the Gordons. It is through their children's success in school that they hope to achieve leverage in their relationship with the Huntleys, that is, an opportunity to establish their equal worth. They have worked hard to finance their children's educations—Mr. Gordon's profits are used for this—and have invested great emotion in their hopes that their children pass exams, get into secondary school, and qualify for white-collar professions. It is the fact that both families send their children to "superior" schools which gives them an added bond of equality. In this light, Dawn Huntley's remark on the road, "You must be disciplined," takes on a new significance. By scolding the Gordon children, two of whom are her own age, telling them that they were "rude" and "facety," * she implied that she, a St. Hilary's girl and a Huntley, would never stoop to such behavior. Although the fact that Louis Huntley had recently passed his exams may have added to the Gordons' resentment, the incident most notably reveals the Gordons' sensitivity to the Huntleys' habitual assertions of superior status, assertions whose legitimacy they do not accept. The Gordons feel that they are as worthy of respect as the Huntleys because they maintain a life style similar to that of the Huntleys, and Mr. Gordon pursues a prestigious occupation, is respected in the community, and his children attend a private preparatory school. In addition, they are related to many respected persons, such as Mr. Gordon's brother in St. Ann's Bay, and a high-level bauxite employee in Coco Hill. Furthermore, the Gordons have a motor vehicle, while the Huntleys do not. Thus, the Gordons feel that the relationship should be one of equality.

To retaliate for real or imagined snubs by the Huntleys, the Gordons tried to lower the Huntleys' prestige in the community. Their insinuation that a man was visiting Dawn at night and that she was therefore behaving in an even more "common" manner than she had attributed to the Gordon children, illustrates this. The story of the Huntley–Gordon dispute was told to me in many versions by different people. Those of lower status than either family, that is, wage laborers and small farmers, sided with the Huntleys. Such people tended to accept their subordinate relationship to the Huntleys because they viewed them as white-collar workers of unquestionably superior status. They could not believe that Dawn would behave in such a manner, and were sure that the rumor was being spread by Mr. Gordon because he

* To act "facety" is to be bold, impudent, impertinent, and rude.

envied the Huntley children's success. Perhaps more important, they were reluctant to accept a subordinate role vis-a-vis Mr. Gordon, whom they remembered from the days when he practiced carpentry, owned no truck or shop, and met them on a more nearly equal level. They resented the fact that he sent his children to private school rather than to school in Coco Hill with their own children, and that it was now necessary for them to come to him for favors and services. They were glad to have an opportunity to vent their hostility toward the Gordons. In contrast, most white-collar workers, big farmers, and entrepreneurs sided with the Gordons. Even though they were unwilling to believe that Dawn Huntley was having an affair with a local man, they were sensitive to the Huntleys' haughty manners, since their own experiences with the family had been similar to those of the Gordons.

The rumor failed, not only because it was widely disbelieved, but because the Huntleys were quite immune to the intended insult. They were not indifferent to the opinion of Coco Hill's white-collar population, but they were more concerned with maintaining their position among other professionals, bauxite employees, and government workers throughout the parish and the entire island. Their status in Coco Hill is secure enough so that they do not depend on the esteem of their neighbors to validate their worth. Although it may have distressed them to some degree to be the butt of a malicious rumor, they attributed it—correctly—to "covetous" feelings on the part of the Gordons. In this way they were able to use the incident to further emphasize their superiority.

After about two months, the incident was smoothed over. Mr. Huntley returned to Mr. Gordon's rum shop and the children from the two families could again be seen romping together on the road. Mr. Huntley ended the feud by apologizing for his daughter's behavior. This did not humiliate him since, in his words, he merely did it to "get back," and he maintains a very patronizing attitude toward the Gordons. The Gordons were willing to accept his gesture of reconciliation, partly because it was made just after the results of the high school admissions exams were announced. The two Huntley girls did not pass the exam, but one of the Gordon girls did. Thus, the relationship was equalized, temporarily at least, and friendly surface relations could be maintained. In fact, the tensions which led to this "fuss" are still present and will probably erupt again when a particular incident brings them to a head.

The Funeral of Joshua Corey

Mrs. Blanche Corey is a 45-year-old black woman who lives on Percy Road, a few houses away from the Gordons and the Huntleys.

She was born in the Cane Road section of the community and comes from a small, independent farming family. Her father owned about five acres of land; he inherited three acres and bought two more with money he earned working on a Cuban sugar estate in the 1920's. Three of Mrs. Corey's brothers and sisters have emigrated to England, one sister is in Kingston doing domestic work, and one remains in Coco Hill. The latter is a housewife and lives with her common-law husband, who owns about three acres of land. Mrs. Corey reached the sixth class at Coco Hill School and then went to a local sewing school. This was a popular but not very lucrative pursuit for girls from farming families in the past. There was not much business in Coco Hill in the first place and when so many girls became dressmakers there was still less demand for each one's services. Soon after completing her training Mrs. Corey went to live with Joshua Corey, a black man from Mitchell Road who was 15 years her senior; they were married shortly after she became pregnant. He had inherited four acres of land from his father, who died when Mr. Corey was a boy. Mr. Corey went to work in the United States in 1945 on the farm contract and saved enough cash to build a house on his land. In 1959 he went to work in England, traveling overseas with Mr. Atwood, a friend from Coco Hill who lived only a few houses away from him. The two shared a room in London where Mr. Corey took various unskilled laboring jobs and worked briefly for London Transport. While he was abroad, he sent regular remittances to his wife who in his absence worked as a clerk in the parish capital (a job she still holds). With money that her husband sent and she herself earned, she bought a new refrigerator, modern furniture, and a television set, and financed her children's education.

Like their mother, the three Corey daughters straighten their hair and wear fashionable store-bought clothing. The eldest daughter, 25, attended secondary school in a nearby town and teaches at a private preparatory school there. The youngest, 17, attends the same secondary school that her sister did, and is a top scholar. She hopes to be admitted to the University of the West Indies to study geography. These two sisters do not socialize with others in Coco Hill; their friends and social life are in a more "cosmopolitan" town. The middle daughter, 22, did not qualify for admission to high school and stays home to help with household chores. She has traveled to the United States on two occasions and plans to emigrate there, to work as a domestic, and to save enough money to send herself to secretarial school.

In October 1968, after having been away for nine years, Mr. Corey returned from England to settle down in Coco Hill. One week later, he was dead of a heart attack. As is so often the case in Coco Hill when someone becomes seriously ill or dies, rumors began to circulate that an obeah man had been paid—in this instance by Mrs. Corey—to set obeah, or magic, on the victim. Underlying this malicious gossip was accumulated hostility which, in the Corey case, was further manifested in nonfulfillment of certain traditional obligations associated with death, such as attending the funeral services and helping to dig the grave.

Many villagers said that Mrs. Corey had been annoyed when her husband returned from England, that she had wanted him to stay there and to continue to send her money. They told me that Mrs. Corey was young-looking and spent money on extravagant clothes but that Mr. Corey had looked weary and haggard, that he had spent the best years of his life toiling and slaving in England.

As in the Huntley–Gordon case, individuals who had a certain type of relationship with Mrs. Corey blamed her for her husband's death. Mrs. Corey is an upwardly mobile person. She comes from a small farming family, but has managed to achieve a life style similar to that of white-collar workers. Her children, especially the youngest girl, have done well in school. While Mrs. Corey has gained the respect and friendship of white-collar workers in Coco Hill, she has been less successful with many of her own relatives and neighbors, who have known her from childhood. Her status, like Mr. Gordon's, depends on a revamping of attitudes toward her; people must come to respect her as a superordinate. In order to achieve this, she has adopted a haughty manner. For instance, villagers are expected to greet one another when they meet on the road; the greeting is more than a mere formality—it symbolizes the existence of a friendly relationship between two people.*
If a person passes by without saying "how-de-do," a slight is communicated which can be grounds for bitter dispute. It is also customary for people having "fuss" to avoid saying hello. Mrs. Corey is noted for frequently passing people on the road—particularly those whom she deems to be of lower status—without saying "how-de-do"; this is taken as an indication of her "proudness."

Mrs. Corey's insecurity in her newly arrived-at position and other villagers' sensitivity to her behavior are displayed in an incident which occurred some years ago. While she and her cousin John White, a landless laborer, were talking, he insulted her. The insult reflected John White's long-felt resentment of Mrs. Corey's haughty demeanor; he expected her to treat him with the respect due a close relative.**

---

     * Merely saying "how-de-do" does not imply equality. Other factors, such as the terms of address and the manner of speaking, serve as indicators of the relative status of the people involved.

     ** The difference in status between the two is clear in the terms of address used by the villagers to refer to each. Mrs. Corey is always referred to as "Miss Blanche" or "Mistress Corey" while her cousin is always called "John" or "John White."

Mrs. Corey was infuriated by his remark; she felt that since she maintained a respectable standard of living and sent her children to high school, John White had no right to conduct himself in this manner. In retaliation, she called him a "dirty nigger." He challenged her, they hurled insulting remarks at each other, and he finally knocked her to the ground. To get revenge, she reported the incident to the police, but they told her that she would need a witness in order to bring legal action. Although three people had seen the incident, they refused to acknowledge it, and tried instead to remain uninvolved. This is common in Coco Hill; people are often reluctant to be dragged into disputes by serving as witnesses to quarrels.* In this particular case, two of the onlookers were partly hidden behind their doors so that Mrs. Corey was unaware that they had seen the fight. They were related to both Mrs. Corey and Mr. White, and did not want to take a stand against either. The third person was on friendly terms with John White and was unwilling to be a witness against him. He told Mrs. Corey that he could not testify because it was a family matter and therefore should be settled out of court. This action earned him Mrs. Corey's hostility, and she still does not speak to him.

John White, in turn, wished to get his revenge and to damage his cousin's reputation, so he took the case to a church court, a common procedure. In this case, Mr. White went to an elder of the Seventh Day Adventist Church, to which Mrs. Corey belongs, and complained of her "ungodly" behavior. The elder conducted an investigation and Mrs. Corey was summoned to an informal trial. She refused to attend and continued her efforts to bring the case to government court, although she was never able to get witnesses to testify. At the same time, John White was infuriated by what he felt was the unfairness of the church court—the officials did not expel Mrs. Corey, as he had hoped they would do, but merely suspended her from the church choir for six months.

The fact that Mrs. Corey went to such great lengths in her battle with her cousin and that she was involved in a dispute with him in the first place, indicates that she is still insecure about her respectability and must constantly assert her superiority to her relatives in Coco Hill.

The hostility that her husband's relatives feel toward her is another factor. Not only do they resent her haughty manner and rise to success, but they feel that Joshua Corey was duped by his wife; while he worked

---

* A person generally agrees to be a witness only if he is on bad terms with the person to be tried. Otherwise, he tries to stay uninvolved. Many informants told me that they would stay behind their doors, anxiously listening to the quarrel, but would not indicate that they had actually been a witness. In other cases, people have been known to "plant" witnesses, asking a friend to hide in the bush to witness a quarrel which they inevitably provoked by some insulting remark.

hard in England, she spent his money freely. Mr. Corey sent most of his savings to his wife rather than to his other relatives in Coco Hill; the latter saw that Mrs. Corey bought more and more furniture, wore fashionable clothing, and sent her children to high school and abroad, and said that she kept money that Mr. Corey meant for them. They did not blame Mr. Corey, who was their relative and was far away, but focused their envy and hostility on his wife, whose origins were no higher than theirs, yet was able to use her situation for her own benefit. The fact that she acted "proud" added to their bitter feelings; her material success and her children's educational attainments remained constant reminders of her superior status. Thus, both her husband's relatives and others in Coco Hill, including many of her own kin, were only too glad to believe that she had caused her husband's death; only a few of her relatives—generally the more successful ones—rallied to her support. They did so partly because the malicious rumor reflected on them and they did not want it said that a member of their family was responsible for Mr. Corey's death.

This widespread hostility was evident at Mr. Corey's funeral, when many people stayed away from the services altogether, a rare occurrence in Coco Hill, where funerals are important social events. People look forward to attending funerals and wearing their best funeral clothes; it is at this time that survivors are expected to show solidarity with each other and respect for the deceased. The success of a funeral depends on its attendance—a successful funeral is one at which there is a "big crowd"—and the prestige of the close kin of the deceased is evaluated on the basis of how many and what kind of people attend. The Corey funeral was poorly attended. Nearly half the seats in the church were empty and the staff of the school where one of the daughters works occupied many of the seats. In one sense this was a source of prestige since the teachers are respected white-collar workers and town dwellers. However, the fact that so few Coco Hill residents appeared was an undeniable slight. Each of the speakers, respected members of the community and elders of the church, referred to the rumors circulating in Coco Hill, and implored "those with sharp tongues to hold back their talk," and to accept the fact that Mr. Corey's death had been the result of a heart attack.

A dispute as to where the body should be buried deepened the resentment felt by Mr. Corey's relatives. Like most families in Coco Hill, they have a family burial plot, and people in the community had assumed that Mr. Corey would be buried in it. However, Mrs. Corey insisted that he be buried in the public plot, about two miles from her home. This bypassing of the family plot angered her husband's relatives. Furthermore, since the public plot is used primarily for "strangers" who have no family in Coco Hill, and very few persons are buried there, Mrs. Corey was relegating her husband to an inferior status in death by burying him outside his family's own plot. Mrs. Corey's enemies said that she was insisting on the public cemetery, farther from her home, because she was afraid that Mr. Corey's duppy, or ghost, would return to haunt her if he were buried close by. In this way they justified their claim that she had indeed set obeah on him and feared his retaliation. As a result of the accumulated bitterness, Mr. Corey's relatives ignored Coco Hill tradition and refused to help dig his grave; Mrs. Corey was forced to hire men in the community to perform this service.

Although the funeral occurred in October 1968, Mrs. Corey was still not speaking to her husband's family a year later.

SOURCES AND NATURE OF DISPUTES

These two incidents reveal certain general patterns which characterize most disputes in the community. They arise when a person claims, or is felt to claim, superior status and when these claims are not regarded as legitimate. One important claim to higher status is the educational success of one's children. This is illustrated by the above cases: both Mrs. Corey and the Huntleys felt that they deserved respect, in large part, because their children were successful in school. In general, when children qualify for secondary school or pass exams, their parents claim deference from status equals, a deference ordinarily accorded only to persons who have a higher status. Thus, there is a disjunction between their claims to deference and their actual status, and this can lead to conflict. Moreover, their claims to deference further reflect the contradiction between the norms of the local social system and the norms of individual achievement in the wider society. On the one hand, villagers want to send their children to secondary school so that the latter can qualify for prestigious and well-paid occupations. On the other hand, they occupy specific status positions and have kinship ties in the local social system which define their expectations about the behavior of others and the behavior expected of them.*

* This discussion parallels Chandra Jayawardena's analysis of eye-pass disputes in a Guianese sugar plantation. The term has its origins in expressions such as "you eye-pass me" or "you take him eye and pass me." To eye-pass someone is to belittle him, to humiliate him, or to ignore his rights and claims. According to Jayawardena, eye-pass disputes are the expression of conflict between the egalitarian norms of the plantation community and the norms of individual achievement in the wider society. The egalitarian ideology proclaims that no man is better than another, that one person deserves what all deserve and that one person's interests are the same as those of another. However, as members of the wider society, individual laborers are motivated to achieve success, acquire culturally valued goods and manners, and to secure upward mobility for their children. See Chandra Jayawardena, *Conflict and Solidarity in a Guianese Plantation* (London: Athlone Press, 1963), pp. 135–141.

A more systematic analysis of disputes in the village, the people involved, and the foci of disputes makes these points clear. What types of persons are most likely to quarrel? Disputes tend to occur between persons who are supposed to treat each other as equals: kin and persons in similar positions in the local status system. When a person is considered a status equal in terms of occupation, land ownership, income, and life style, or is a close kinsman, any claims to superiority which he makes, or is felt to make, are not regarded as legitimate.

The status ranking of an individual is also affected by age and disputants are usually close in age. For the purposes of this discussion five age groups appear to be important: children under nine; children in the upper grades of primary school; young people who have left school but who have not entered into regular domestic unions; those who have domestic responsibilities of their own but whose children have not yet started to work; older people.[3] Persons at these different stages of the life cycle are expected to achieve different status levels. This is modified by their position, or the position of their parents, in the local status system. Thus it is expected that the son of a big farmer will be more successful than the son of a wage laborer. However, within status groups, persons of the same age are expected to have achieved similar status. For example, a man under 30 is not expected to own much land or to be fully established in an occupation; a person in his 40's is. The young man recognizes the older man's claims to status as legitimate and treats him with respect since the young man feels that he himself has not yet had the opportunity to achieve such success. But an individual is not considered subordinate to a contemporary who is a close kinsman or the child of parents of similar status, even if the age-peer is more successful than he.

Kinship relations add further complexity to the analysis. Kinsmen, by the very fact of their kinship, are considered equals, although they may be in different status positions. Disputes among them thus reflect the conflict between two sets of local norms, that is, the norms which define behavior between kin and those which define behavior between persons in different statuses in the village. Since most persons have wide kinship networks in the community, most are related to persons in different status groups. On the one hand, they are supposed to treat relatives as equals and to fulfill certain obligations to them. On the other hand, if they are of a higher status in the local status system than certain kin, they may feel that they should be treated with added respect. The conflict between these sets of norms is clear in the case of Mrs. Corey and her cousin, John White. Mrs. Corey's haughty behavior to her cousin violated the norms which define their relationship as an equal one. In retaliation, John White insulted Mrs. Corey, a violation on his part of the norms which dictate that since his cousin is accepted by many white-collar workers in the community as an equal he should treat her with a certain amount of respect.

To sum up, disputes often break out between putative status equals when one makes claims to higher status. The actual eruption of disputes is affected by another factor, however; quarrels tend to occur between persons who have regular social interactions with each other, such as neighbors, church brethren, or fellow teachers. Even though a villager may recognize the value of another's achievement—for example, sending a child to secondary school—he remains sensitive to real or imagined slights from such persons, particularly if he or his children have not been successful. He feels the need to assert his equal worth, and often does so through retaliatory actions.

This is further illustrated by another example. Mrs. Anglin is a 43-year-old black woman whose husband cultivates two acres of land and operates a small stone quarry. He occasionally hires a man to help him in the quarry, but is deep in debt to the bank since he borrowed money to purchase the quarry land and to buy the necessary equipment. Mrs. Anglin, a higgler, is an active member of the Church of God—unlike her husband who rarely attends services. Mrs. Anglin has been trying to see that her eldest daughter, Alda, 16, "gets on." She prods her to study to pass the Jamaica School Certificate Examinations but Alda is not a good scholar. Mrs. Anglin is continually engaged in disputes with other women whose children have been successful in their exams and schooling. For instance, she had a big "fuss" with a neighbor, the wife of a small farmer, with whom she was quite friendly. Alda had told her mother that the neighbor's daughter had not only made fun of her in class, taunting her about how she was too "dunce" to pass the exams, but had also claimed that Alda was not a true Christian—a great slight since Alda accompanies her mother regularly to the services at the Church of God. Mrs. Anglin complained to me:

> Some of them go on like they're better than others. They just feel proud. It leave to their action, the way they act with you and your children who can't go there [to secondary school]. Because their child is pushing it up and yours is down. A proudness to them. For example, you and a person may used to move well and go to that person and after a while that person show you a funny face and you wouldn't feel to go to that person home again. You have plenty proud people in Coco Hill. I don't try to skin my nose up at people. I have my children and am trying with them. I feel proud in my heart but not acting that way with people. Just trying my best. Some of them feel proud when the

child is doing good work at school but them should only give God thanks.

Even if the people she has had "fuss" with have not acted "proud" or boasted of their children's achievements, Mrs. Anglin feels that because her children have been less successful, the others have assumed a superior and haughty air. She also feels that they openly or covertly ridicule her because her children are not "pushing it up," something which deeply hurts Mrs. Anglin because she works so hard for her children. She goes to market three times a week, even when sick, and insists on washing her children's clothes (Mrs. Anglin has seven sons, all younger than Alda) every day so that they will look "nice on the road." She has recently acquired a sewing machine and takes pride in sewing dresses for herself and her daughter. The life style that she and her family maintain, the income that they have, and the occupations which both she and her husband follow place them in an equal status position to a number of people in the district whose children have done well in school. Mrs. Anglin is quick to take offense at any actual or felt slight from these persons and to vent her anger through some retaliatory action. She does not deny that their children's educational success is a significant achievement. However, she feels that since her status is equal to theirs, they have no right to claim superiority. She has "traced," or cursed, a woman whose son had insulted one of her children; she poisoned the fowl of a "boasty" neighbor who is now in the United States but whose children were then in secondary school; she brought a woman to church court who, she claimed, had been spreading false rumors about Alda. Through such actions she is able to vent some of her hostility and to assert her "righteousness" and superiority to people who have, according to her, resorted to malicious gossip to enhance their prestige at her expense.

Other examples suggest that the particular incident which triggers a quarrel may seem relatively trivial or unrelated to the underlying cause of the dispute. In the case of the Huntleys and the Gordons, it was Dawn Huntley's remarks on the road which led to the quarrel. In another case, Mr. Hall, a small farmer, became enraged because a neighbor's fowl ate up his crops. He reacted by poisoning the offending fowl, which in turn infuriated the neighbor. The poisoning of the fowl was not only a reaction to crop damage but reflected—as was indicated to me in many conversations—Mr. Hall's jealousy of the success of his neighbor's children and his sensitivity to that neighbor's "boasty" behavior. In a case where jealousy and injured feelings had not been involved, the aggrieved party might merely have asked the neighbor to take measures to restrain the fowl. One enterprising young girl in the village responded to insults from a schoolmate by writing to the request program on one of the island's two radio stations. She asked the disc jockey to play the song "Snake in the Grass," prefaced by the message "Greetings to Blanche in Coco Hill. Stop beating round my bush."

OBEAH

Obeah is another important means of expressing hostility toward people who acquire valued consumption items or whose children are successful in school. Obeah threats and accusations are used in the course of many disputes, and some villagers also accuse individuals of higher status of using obeah to achieve their positions. The term "obeah" encompasses the set of beliefs and practices associated with the magical powers of certain men and women. They are called obeah men or women, and are thought to have the power to send duppies, or the spirits of the dead, to harm the living. They are consulted in times of sickness, misfortune in farming or business, crossed love, or other troubles. Such difficulties are often attributed to the fact that another villager has set obeah on them, that is, gone to an obeah man.

Obeah is viewed as the cause of misfortune when natural causes cannot be pinpointed, and to explain why a particular misfortune strikes a particular person at a particular time. As one woman told me:

> For instance I have a pig dead and I know nobody hurt it. Pig can have fever and other disease. If you have three pigs and them all die, you feel God wouldn't take all three pigs like that. When you find the goat just lie down dead, it isn't hang, nobody hit it, it has no sickness, you have to wonder what happened. Is when someone sick and doctor can't see what wrong. Say nothing wrong with you. Some doctor say can't find your complaining. Is then you have to try somewhere else [obeah man].

Obeah men can help their clients to achieve success and they can also bring retribution to one's enemies. For a high price, often as much as £15, they give their clients certain objects and potions which, when buried on the victim's land or worn in a certain way, act on the intended victim. They also frequently make long lists of items that the client must buy at a pharmacy, items to cause the spirits of the dead to work harm on the living.

As far as I know, there was no obeah man resident in Coco Hill when I lived in the community, although one obeah man had lived on Percy Road several years before I came to Coco Hill. I had at first thought that the villagers might hesitate to admit to me that an obeah

man lived in the community, since obeah is illegal, and both obeah
men and those who seek their services are liable to prosecution.* However, people showed no reluctance to tell me about other illegal aspects
of life in Coco Hill, such as who the major growers of "ganja," or
marihuana, were. I also supposed that the villagers might be ashamed
to tell me about obeah, since it is looked down upon by most respectable white-collar workers in the community as a superstition, but the
same people who told me about "ganja"-growers were willing to tell
me who the noted "warner men" were, that is, men who have visions
and warn their neighbors of future catastrophes, an equally looked-
down-upon and superstitious practice.

People in Coco Hill are said to go to Spanish Town and to villages
in other parishes, particularly St. Thomas, to consult obeah men:
"Them take them car and hire car and go far away . . . I don't hear
them say any here in Coco Hill. In St. Thomas and other far places."
The fact that people have to travel to consult obeah men adds to the
mystique surrounding the practice by making it a major undertaking.
In addition, the obeah man, supposedly unfamiliar with the intricacies
of social relations in Coco Hill, is believed to have superhuman powers
because he can tell who set obeah on his client.** Moreover, going far
away makes it easier to conceal the visits, something which many
villagers want to do because obeah is not considered an entirely respectable practice. People in Coco Hill often did not want to admit
to me that they actually believed in obeah. In fact, white-collar workers
use their disdain of obeah as another mark of their superior status.
However, once most villagers got involved in explaining obeah to me
and telling me of various incidents, it became obvious that they did
believe that obeah had caused certain misfortunes to other persons
or was responsible for the success of other villagers and they would
become animated in the course of recounting the tales.

Whether a person actually believes in the efficacy of obeah or
has sought an obeah man at one time in his life, obeah serves as the
idiom through which all in the village openly discuss hostilities. For
example, the teacher I lived with did not believe in obeah and neither
did I. Yet every time someone in the village died we were anxious to
know who had been "accused" of the death and could usually predict
who the person was before the "official" report reached us. For the
next few days, the major topic of conversation in most homes revolved

---

* Obeah men often pay off the local police, and obeah is unofficially tolerated.
** Often the obeah man has informants in the communities from which his
clients come and knows whom to blame for misfortunes. People in Coco Hill also
seem to frequent the same obeah men.

around the "causes" of the death, the relationship between the deceased and the "accused," and the envy and jealousy which caused the "accused" to set obeah. Similarly, people use the obeah accusations of others to support their own dislike of a person, whether they actually believe in obeah or not.

Nearly every informant said that it was more successful people who went to obeah men and one of the most frequent reasons given was that parents wanted their children to succeed in school. Moreover, many felt that parents of successful children had used obeah to block the academic success of others' children:

> Obeah? Some say they will make you have work and get money. Some people believe them. Even educated people. Some believe they can help the children pass exam. But you have to study the thing. Are foolish people who believe in that. Child who is well fed can stay up half the night to study.

> Obeah? Bible say workers of iniquity but me don't worry about it. Anything me want, me just work hard for it. I love people work hard, but some people give in to obeah and try all kind of plan. People must sick, failure must come. . . . Some people do not try to help themself and when them not in certain position feels is obeah that makes them not like the other person. Some people, all must be in the same nice house and all the children should pass exams. But is not all the children have the brain. Some children have no ambition and they think it obeah. Say is the children who passing the exam who put obeah on them.

> Like if you going to take an exam, some people say that they gonna work obeah on you. I hear a man up the hill, Mr. Richardson, goes to a man every night and work obeah on other people. That's how his children go to school and pass exam.

> If you have a child who doesn't do anything, does bad in school and take that child to the doctor and he says nothing is wrong and you believe someone obeah him. My son, he talk a whole lot of foolishness, stares in space, and we know he loves his book and talk about school all the time. Needs must be someone set obeah . . .

> Many people suffering from that, not I personally. They just covetous and feel you shouldn't be the one. That child profession will allow his or her parents to come up. If he cripples that child, prosperity. When they are going to envy you, generally say they are going to an obeah man. For instance, if I find Winston get funny and take him to a place [obeah man] is the most I can do to help him.

> The children at school, at exam time, they won't lend their book

to each other. They believe that the one they lend it to, put a curse on the book. They say that when they get the book back their eyes go dark and they cannot study and they fail the exams.

Thus, successful persons are accused of using obeah to achieve certain desired goals and to hinder the success of others. In fact, one of the respondents could not understand why an obeah man would even want to help anyone. She reasoned that if a person had these magical powers, then he would hoard them for his own benefit. Persons who are quarrelling frequently threaten to set obeah on their enemy and accuse their enemy of having resorted to obeah to "strike them down."

As with disputes and quarrels, a person generally blames his mis-fortunes and bad luck on someone of his own status or a kinsman who has, or is felt to have, slighted him by claiming superior status. How-ever, unlike disputes, obeah also expresses hostility across status-group lines and in situations in which the two are not related by ties of kinship. Thus, one works obeah on persons of approximately the same status but one is accused of this action by persons of both inferior and superior status. For example, a poor wage laborer does not usually quarrel with a big farmer and maintains an outward air of deference to him. If the wage laborer is struck by a misfortune he does not blame a big farmer but feels that it is the doing of another wage laborer or kinsman who has been more successful than he. But he also explains the success of big farmers and white-collar workers in terms of obeah.

Obeah threats and accusations do not operate as effective sanc-tions against "boasty" behavior since the desire to attain socially valued symbols of prestige is more powerful than the fear that one's success will meet with hostility and obeah accusations from others. Most vil-lagers are aware that their fellows are "covetous" and "envious" and "don't want to see anyone else get on":

> If you do good, people talk. If you do bad, people talk. So just do good and let people talk. They chat you anyway, do all manner of evil.

Those most often accused of "boasty" behavior and obeah by others are upwardly mobile villagers like Mrs. Corey and Mr. Gordon. These persons assume a superior air to many in the community and often boast of their achievements. They do not want the friendship, but the respect, of those whom they regard as inferior in status and they therefore violate many of the local norms which regulate be-havior, such as saying "how-de-do" to those they pass on the road. A good example of this is Mr. Richardson, son of a successful small farmer. He works at one of the bauxite companies, owns 10 acres of land, a big house and a car, and has sent two of his children to university and three to teacher training college. Mr. Richardson frequently boasts of the achievements of his children and the material possessions he has purchased and is therefore accused of resorting to obeah. Villagers told me that he went to an obeah man every night and when another bauxite employee died, Mr. Richardson was accused of the death. He is concerned with establishing his status position in the community, and in part, his "proudness" reflects his assumed air of not caring what the "common" and "ordinary" people in Coco Hill think of him. He explains that he is accused of obeah because the villagers envy his achievements and in this way he uses the accusations to further validate his claims to status.

SANCTIONS

It is true that there are numerous sanctions which induce persons to conform to local norms and thus to refrain from boasting of their own or their children's achievements, but these sanctions are not always effective. The desire to claim prestige on the basis of one's children's success is often more powerful than the fear of being the butt of local gossip, of being taken to church or government court, of losing the reciprocity of kin and neighbors, or of being denied certain favors such as loans of money or labor. Even when individuals do not emphasize their good fortune by claiming deference on such a basis, they are often envied merely because their children have been more successful than those of kin and neighbors.

Thus, many in Coco Hill are not "boasty" and are sensitive to the norms which define the behavior that status equals and kin expect of them. They know who is offended if they talk about their children's achievements and who is not. For example, Mrs. Martin, wife of a small farmer, often talked about her son's plans to become an engineer in front of a poor woman, the common-law wife of a cane cutter. The latter respects Mrs. Martin because Mrs. Martin lives in a nice house, her husband is fairly successful, and her son goes to technical high school. In contrast, Mrs. Martin usually tempers her talk of her son's ambitions when speaking to her peers, and she is very popular with the wives of other small farmers in the district. Nonetheless, even when women like Mrs. Martin are not "boasty," their behavior is often interpreted as such merely because their children are successful.

A person seldom claims deference on the basis of his children's success in school from those who are of a higher status in the community. For example, a small farmer who sends his child to secondary school does not expect deference from a big farmer, since he recognizes that his own inferior position does not vary solely according to his child's achievements.

Education is, of course, only one basis of "fuss" in the community, and villagers quarrel when there are other factors which give, or are felt to give, a person of similar status or a kinsman a claim to superior status. For example, many disputes are rooted in the fact that a person has acquired a valued consumption item such as a refrigerator, television set, or sewing machine, and, as in the disputes which stem from the educational achievements of children, the quarrel may arise over a seemingly unrelated incident.

RESOLUTION OF DISPUTES

Some disputes continue for years, with the antagonists avoiding any kind of interaction. In one case a woman refused even to ride in the same bus with an enemy of 10 years' standing, but most quarrels do not last this long. Some are settled in a few days, others after several months. Almost always, friendly relations are eventually resumed —in the words of the villagers, the parties "get back"—but the incidents are rarely forgotten. Feelings of mistrust and anxiety generally underly the relationship, and there is fear of a new quarrel arising from another, possibly related, conflict. Since the basis for most quarrels is the success of one of the disputants, this fear is well-grounded, and was evident in the kinds of disputes the villagers were willing to discuss with me. While most of them were willing to tell me about quarrels that were taking place at the time, few would discuss settled disputes in which they had been involved. They feared that the other party would hear that they had been "talking bad" about them to me, would take offense, and begin the quarrel again.

Since most disputes in the community occur between persons who frequently interact with one another as social equals, and who depend on each other for favors and services, there is usually a resolution of differences and a reestablishment of friendly relations. A number of pressures lead to settlement of disputes. Those who quarrel are often neighbors, church brethren, persons who live in the same house, or kin. It is hard to keep up a state of war with someone who cannot be avoided and on whom one depends for services. Moreover, since Coco Hill is a small community and since villagers are interrelated by many ties, one's friends, neighbors, and kin are usually on friendly terms with one's enemy. Therefore, the disputants interact on friendly terms with the same people, who are generally hesitant to become involved in the "fuss" and sometimes try to settle the quarrel.

There are several informal means for settling disputes. Often one of the disputants apologizes to the other, or he continues to say "how-de-do" when they meet on the road until the other person answers. In many cases the person who was originally perceived as claiming superior status settles the dispute by apologizing or making other conciliatory gestures. In a sense, this equalizes the relationship, since he is asking for forgiveness and admitting that he erred. However, the fact that he has been more successful may lead to future "fuss." In other cases, the two parties make peace by blaming a third party for spreading the rumors that gave rise to a quarrel. In these instances, the settlement of one dispute may lead to a new one.

The villagers also have access to two formal methods of settling disputes—government and church courts. However, both procedures merely intensify disputes and are used by the villagers to lower the status of their enemy, and thus to justify their own status claims. Many villagers resort to government court despite the fact that lawyers' fees can amount to as much as £15. In fact, willingness to initiate court action is a symbol of prestige because it is so expensive. A person who is slighted by another villager often takes him to the government court, located in a nearby town, to prove that he can afford to redress the wrong done to him, and thus affirms his status. Although disputants sometimes apologize after a court case is held, hostile feelings are more often heightened. Moreover, a witness is usually needed and this involves a third party in the quarrel. Often a person who is taken to government court retaliates by complaining to a church court, as John White did after Mrs. Corey tried to bring him to the government court.

Every church in Coco Hill has a court. Each church court hears only cases in which its members are the defendants, although the complainants may or may not be members of this church. In addition, the complaint must involve a question of Christian morality. The elected officials of the church (in the case of the Pentecostal Church and the Church of God, the resident ministers) serve as judges. Since the ministers in the Pentecostal Church and the Church of God are "strangers" to Coco Hill, many more villagers resort to these church courts than to those of the other churches, where the judges are natives of the community and therefore linked by friendship, kinship, and residence to those they try. Their judgment is viewed as less objective by the villagers and they are, in fact, less willing to try cases lest they become embroiled in disputes with their friends and relatives. Thus, for example, the Baptist Tabernacle Church hears four or five cases a year, while the Church of God minister told me that about 10 people a month come to him with complaints about members, and approximately 35 cases end up in his church's court each year.

The courts are formally held so that grievances against members can be aired before church elders rather than before the government magistrates. In this way, it is hoped, the dispute will be settled peacefully and privately. However, the major power of the church courts is that they can publicly embarrass a member by putting him on probation or dismissing him from the church and accusing him of behavior unworthy of a true Christian and church member. Although the church trials are supposed to be private affairs, most villagers know the details of the proceedings, and taking someone to church court exacerbates, rather than settles, a dispute. Moreover, the person who is judged guilty often becomes angry at the leaders or officials who try the case and this may lead to new disputes.

The case of Mrs. Grant, an active church member, reveals how the church court process works. Mrs. Grant, a brown-skinned woman of 27, is a "stranger" to Coco Hill, married to a truck driver at a bauxite company. Her husband's salary is relatively high by Coco Hill standards and the couple rents two well-furnished rooms in a home with a private catchment tank. Mrs. Grant straightens her hair, usually wears store-bought clothes, and regularly attends the JSC classes. She hopes to pass the JSC exams and qualify for secretarial training.

A dispute originated when Mrs. Cooper, a neighbor, accused Mrs. Grant of having an affair with her husband, a teacher. She complained that one night she had found her husband at Mrs. Grant's home and that Mrs. Grant was wearing only a nightgown. To get her revenge, Mrs. Cooper spoke to two of the elders at Mrs. Grant's church, and Mrs. Grant was summoned to court:

> They send to call me and on Thursday night I go up there. Just those elders and myself and the Pastor. Six of us. The officers were seated on the benches and I was seated on a chair and Pastor on a chair. The Pastor say, "Sister Grant, a report came to me about you, that you have been friendly with another man. What do you say to that?" Then he say, "Wait a bit" and ask Brown to speak. Brown [an elder] said that Mrs. Cooper said to him that Cooper was coming to see me quite regular and that she will have to find some way to stop him. Pastor then ask the next elder to talk and he say the same thing. After that Pastor says, "What do you have to say?" I said, "The fact is that the teacher gave him the English assignment to give to me. His wife came and fetched him." I said to him, "Pastor you are out of order because I was sick." Pastor says, "The best place to entertain a nonmember is on the verandah." I tell him, "They are not going to tell me where I take anybody in my house." They say I am out of order. They building up something against me. I told them that I had to leave because my husband was going to work and they tell me that I am on

probation and I left. The next Wednesday the elder Brown come to tell me that I was to meet the Parson and the officers at the church on Wednesday night and I say I am busy and not coming. The next day I meet another member of the church and he tell me that they call my name Wednesday night and that I am no longer a member of the church. I don't talk to Brown or to the other elder who spoke to me. And I don't talk to Parson or his wife either.

Mrs. Grant still bears Mrs. Cooper a grudge, but she is even more angry with the church elders and the minister. In her eyes the church elders are of a lower status than she and her husband, since they are only small farmers. Therefore, she feels that they have no right to pass judgment on her behavior. She feels her standing is equal to the minister's because her life style is similar to his; Mrs. Grant attributes the minister's behavior to his resentment of her social position. She told me that the minister wants all of the church members to defer to him and that she refuses to do so because she is not inferior to him. In this case, clearly, the church court did not settle the dispute and indeed, created a new "fuss" between Mrs. Grant and the church officials.

CONCLUSION

Disputes in Coco Hill are a medium for the expression of status envy among villagers. In somewhat parallel fashion, obeah threats and accusations are also an important medium through which hostilities toward successful villagers are expressed. It is true that there are other ways in which the villagers release their frustrations and disappointments—for example, woundings, drinking, and hostility toward national political leaders. Further, some do not accept disappointment but search for other avenues of mobility, such as going to work abroad. However, disputes and obeah accusations provide a major outlet for the expression of discontent. It follows from this, I would argue, that such local conflicts are an important means of reducing cleavages at the national level, for they permit individuals to vent their frustrated mobility aspirations onto other persons in the local social system. This is an alternative to questioning the values of the national society which determine status criteria, challenging the legitimacy of the institutions which provide only limited channels to mobility, or participating in open conflict against established authorities.

PART 3

Politics

VII

Political Organization

I have discussed the role of education in facilitating mobility within Jamaican society, changes in the society which have led to the expansion of the educational system, and certain consequences of these changes in the daily lives of people in a rural community. We shall now consider another major institutional complex which, at the national level at least, affects the stratification system. In this chapter and the one to follow I consider the local political structure, what opportunities it provides for social mobility through political office and patronage, and the importance of politics as a factor in social relationships.

The advent of independence and the emergence of modern political parties and their trade union affiliates have produced many changes on the island. Rural villagers have never had local formal authority structures such as village councils and have always been part of a centralized political system. But prior to 1944, they were effectively disenfranchised because of literacy and property qualifications and were thereby excluded from the formal political processes of the island. Even for those who could vote, the power of the ballot was severely circumscribed from 1866 until 1944. After the assumption of Crown Colony government in 1866, the Crown-appointed Governor held all effective political power in the country.* He presided over what was in 1866 a 12-man Legislative Council of nominated and ex-officio members. Constitutional reforms in 1884 and 1895 added elected members to the Council, but these members were still a minority on a body that could not initiate legislation. The white and colored elites elected to the Council did not favor popular government, for fear of the potential power of the black masses, and they sought to influence the Governor in order to promote their own business and agricultural interests. As for the parish boards, abolished in 1866, they were re-stored in 1885 as elected bodies; but they had a minimum of functions and were dependent on the central government for grants-in-aid.

During the Crown Colony era, the Colonial Office considered that one of its roles was to represent the "unrepresented" classes in Jamaica and to this end it made some economic and social improvements. How-ever, there were no effective, legitimate political means through which rural villagers could fight for more far-reaching economic and prestige goals or express their mobility aspirations. Since the emergence in the 1940's of a democratic two-party system based on universal adult suffrage, the rural villagers have been able to participate in the politi-cal institutions of the nation.

The political parties and their trade union affiliates provide new vocational roles for individuals in the society, and the parties distribute benefits to their supporters in the form of patronage and preferment for appointments in government service. Moreover, there has been a shift in the ideological basis of politics. The imperial government insti-tutionalized the idea that persons should be allocated to positions and judged on the basis of merit. However, colonial political elites did not provide equal opportunities for lower classes to advance in the social system and did not allow them to vote. In contrast, the post-World War II national political leaders of both parties stress that all members of the society should have equal opportunities for achieve-

---

* The Jamaican Assembly, an elected body, was a key power center prior to 1865, when some 400 ex-slaves led by Paul Bogle, a Baptist deacon, came down from the hills to the town of Morant Bay to protest a decision by local magistrates. This protest was only a small expression of the pent-up feelings of injustice among the ex-slaves; the settlers complained of the shortage of land, the difficulty of finding wage employment, the absence of an impartial judiciary, and their poor living conditions. The clash at Morant Bay led to the killing of 21 whites and 9 blacks; in the suppression that followed throughout the island, 439 blacks were killed, 600 were flogged, and 1,000 houses were burned. A colored member of the Assembly, George William Gordon, bitter critic of the Governor and friend of Bogle's, was hanged for his alleged role in the "rebellion." Fearful of future uprisings and the potential political power of the black masses, the Assembly surrendered its constitution and accepted Crown Colony government. See Philip Curtin, *Two Jamaicas: The Role of Ideas in a Tropical Colony, 1830–1865* (Cambridge: Harvard University Press, 1955) and Hall, *op. cit.*

ment and that the government should be responsive to the "will of the people."

Before discussing how these structural and ideological changes have affected the lives of the villagers of Coco Hill, it is helpful to give a brief account of the national structure of Jamaica's political parties.

MODERN POLITICAL PARTIES

The development of modern political parties and their trade union affiliates dates from the riots and disturbances of 1938.* In response to these disturbances, which occurred throughout the West Indies, the British government sent out a destroyer, followed by a Royal Commission to the West Indies, under the chairmanship of Lord Moyne. This commission recommended the creation of a West Indian Welfare Fund, the extension of suffrage, and the establishment of trade unions, labor departments, a minimum wage, and workmen's compensation. These recommendations became the foundation for the post-war Colonial Development and Welfare Acts and set a pattern for self-government demands throughout the British Empire.

The 1938 disturbances provided a political tool for aspiring members of the creole elite, who were beginning to challenge the legitimacy of English rule. They had qualified for prestigious occupations and yet were denied access to top administrative and political posts in the society. Individuals in this group did not base their appeal on nationalist ideals, and argued instead that cultural "whiteness" rather than ethnic "whiteness" should be the criterion of high status. They continued to think of themselves as very different from the mass of the population below them. As Raymond Smith writes:

* Mob action, bloodshed, property damage, declaration of martial law, and the arrest of ringleaders characterized these disturbances. Prior to this, a number of factors had exacerbated the poor conditions of the black lower classes: rising unemployment with the fall in world prices for Jamaican exports; increased awareness of deprivation stemming from reports of migrants returned from the United States and Central America, and the spread of education and communications in the early part of the century. Excluded from participation in the formal political system and denied collective bargaining to air their grievances, they could express their interests and exert pressure on authorities only through illegal means. The disturbances occurred in various parts of the island among laborers on banana and sugar estates and in the public works department, ex-servicemen who had been settled on land grants, and dockers and other members of the Kingston working class. They were sparked by such incidents as reductions in pay, the introduction of "outside" workers from nearby villages, lay-offs on public works projects, and provocative actions by the police. See O. W. Phelps, "The Rise of the Labour Movement in Jamaica," *Social and Economic Studies*, IX (December, 1960), 417–467, and K. W. J. Post, "The Politics of Protest in Jamaica, 1938," *Social and Economic Studies*, XVIII (December, 1969), 374–390.

The problem in the West Indies was, partly at least, that the creole elite had no ideological position on which they could build a separate style of life in opposition to that of the dominant group. . . . In fact one may say that they had no basis for the legitimisation of their position except their similarity to Englishmen. In this sense the Caribbean elite was unlike educated princes, Government chiefs or westernized samurai, and Caribbean nationalism has always lacked the coherent form that might have been supplied by a traditional culture. This has not necessarily been a disadvantage but it does distinguish new world societies from those of Europe, Asia and Africa.[1]

Some members of the creole elite had been active in political reform movements of the 1930's.* After the disturbances of 1938 they realized that any political power they might have was linked to their potential role as spokesmen for the masses, who were felt by the British to represent a major threat to the stability of the social system. For this reason, as some leaders of the creole elite began to agitate for independence, they united with those who had been active in trade union organizing.** At this time two of modern Jamaica's most important political figures, Norman Washington Manley and Sir Alexander Bustamante, emerged, and the modern political parties were formed.

Bustamante made his first appearance during the labor disturbances of the late 1930's as the leader of the working classes. He encouraged the strikers with rousing speeches and was a central figure in many disorders until he was arrested and charged with sedition and inciting unlawful assembly. His arrest merely enhanced his popularity and, although a fair-skinned man, be became the hero of the discontented black workers. He had spent much of his early life away from the island, traveling to Spain, the United States, England, and Latin America; he returned to Jamaica in 1932 to become the proprietor of a small loan business. Bustamante's initial effort was to build a success-

---

* For example, the Jamaica Progressive League, formed in New York City by a group of Jamaican emigrants and headed by the novelist Adolphe Roberts, aimed to implement universal adult suffrage, party activity, and the final goal of dominion status for Jamaica. In 1936 the periodical *Public Opinion* was founded in Kingston by a group of middle-class intellectuals and the National Reform Association was formed in 1937 to press for universal adult suffrage and a higher elective component in the Legislative Council. See Richard Hart, "Jamaica and Self-Determination, 1660–1970," *Race*, XIII (January, 1972), 284–285.

** Trade unions had been legalized in 1919 after a series of riots and strikes in 1918 among dock workers, fire fighters, cane workers, and coal and banana carriers. However, the 1919 law did not grant the right to strike, nor did it establish collective bargaining procedures, and in 1938 only a small percentage of the labor force was organized. See Phelps, *op. cit.*, p. 418.

ful trade union movement; he was the founder, leader, and life president of the Bustamante Industrial Trade Union and he was not directly involved in the movement toward self-government.

In contrast, Norman Manley, an Oxford-educated barrister, was
directly involved in the independence movement. He was a leader of
the People's National Party (PNP), a group formed by left-wing intellectuals in 1938, which by the 1940's advocated immediate independence and adopted a socialist label. Although "Busta" had alternating
periods of friendliness and hostility toward the PNP, he and Manley
cooperated with each other at first. With the approach of the 1944
elections, and the prize of real political power at stake, a sharp split
between the two developed. Bustamante, in jail for sedition, charged
on his release in 1942 that the PNP leaders had conspired to prolong
his detention. He left the party and took his union with him, forming
the Jamaica Labour Party (JLP), which went on to win the elections.

Since 1944, when the first general elections based on universal
adult suffrage were held, the People's National Party and the Jamaica
Labour Party have dominated Jamaican politics.[2] Jamaica has witnessed a relatively untroubled transition from colony to independent
nation, a status it achieved in 1962. The Constitution of 1944 provided
the basic framework for formal governmental structures around which
the political system of the new nation was shaped.[*]

As in all new states, independence has introduced into the society
"a valuable new prize over which to fight."[3] In Jamaica, however,
because there are no long-established tribal ties, for example, to which
politicians might appeal for support, and the population is overwhelmingly black,[**] the cultural and racial cleavages exploited by politicians
in many new states are not operative. Nor has the major division in
Jamaican society—class—become the basis for political division. Originally the two parties did appeal to different classes in the society.
The PNP started out primarily as a middle-class party, drawing its
main support from the urban middle classes to whom Manley represented the image of a very successful man. The Jamaica Labour Party
originally drew its support from the lower classes, sugar workers in

[*] See J.B. Kelly, "The Jamaican Independence Constitution of 1962," *Caribbean Studies*, III (April, 1963). The Jamaican government is based on a cabinet system with an elected lower house from which the ministers are drawn and to which they are responsible. The Prime Minister heads the government and the Governor-General is titular head of state. The Senate, the upper house, is nominated in part by the Prime Minister and in part by the Leader of the Opposition.

[**] Percentage Distribution of People in Jamaica by Racial Composition (Census of 1960)—Africans: 76.3; Afro-Europeans: 15.1; Europeans: 0.8; Chinese/Afro-Chinese: 1.2; East Indians/Afro-East Indians: 3.4; others: 3.2.

particular. Despite its labor base, it was a more conservative party than the PNP, which had initially advocated left-wing policies. The JLP proposed reforms to improve the conditions of the working class within the framework of the existing economic and social institutions, and for this reason it was preferred by the old upper classes and by the sugar companies. However, a combination of factors has caused the two parties to become similar in policy, leadership, and composition, and the major difference between them today is one of style.

One of the most important reasons for this similarity is the need of both parties to win the support of the lower classes who constitute the vast majority of the electorate. Since the 1940's the PNP has made attempts to win support among workers and small farmers. Despite its good political organization, the PNP won few seats in the first national election (1944). As a consequence it recognized the need to develop a wider political base among the working classes, and proceeded to build an organization, the Trade Union Council, to rival the Labour Party's Bustamante Industrial Trade Union. Although the party did acquire some mass support in the urban and rural areas, as a result of such factors as cold war politics, internal leadership struggles, and fear of losing electoral support, it shed many of its more radical policies by the 1950's.* When it assumed power in 1955, it adopted a program of "industrialization by invitation," closely modeled after Munoz Marin's Puerto Rican Operation Bootstrap.

Another factor in the modification of both parties' programs is the fact that both have been in power, and have had to adjust to the exigencies of actually holding office. The PNP, which ruled from 1955 to 1962, and won the 1972 election, had to consider the interests of American and Canadian companies rather than its previous anti-imperialist platform; the JLP, in power from 1944 to 1955 and from 1962 to 1972, found that it had to work with the civil service and, in order to maintain popular support, to continue the welfare programs formulated by its PNP predecessors.

The Labour Party has retained much of its mass backing and has also won support among the middle classes. In addition, it has attracted members of the intelligentsia into its leadership. Thus, both parties not only seek support from the same mass base, but in effect

---

* The defeat of the PNP in 1944 strengthened its left wing, which had argued that the PNP should widen its base to draw in the working classes. In 1951, when the PNP won the local elections, the right wing of the party, afraid that the left wing was becoming too powerful, capitalized on the cold war and insisted that the party expel its "reds" to avoid becoming Communist-dominated. Manley sided with the right wing, expelled the heads of the Trade Union Council, and formed the National Workers' Union.

their policies have been substantially the same. As Gordon K. Lewis perceptively remarks, "although the PNP styled itself socialist, while consistently refusing to give it a Jamaican definition, and the JLP styled itself the defender of capitalism without comprehending the implications of laissez-faire economics in an immature tropical economy, both of them, when saddled with the responsibility to govern, adopted roughly similar methods to attain roughly similar ends." [4] Both parties agreed on the form that self-government should take, removing the island's political status from the arena of party politics. The one issue which did divide the two was the Federation issue of 1961: the PNP advocated Jamaica's joining the Federation of the West Indies and the JLP took an isolationist stand. However, this difference did not create a permanent rift between the two and, once the Federation collapsed, they joined together in a common front at the final independence conference in London in 1962, agreeing on the terms of the Independence Constitution. [5]

The impact of the political party system on Jamaican society has been felt in the nation's social as well as political life. The creation of new leadership positions, both in the parties and in the government itself, has opened a new avenue of mobility.* Although many political leaders are still drawn from the ranks of the creole elite—that is, professionals and civil servants—a number have risen through the party and trade union ranks to achieve important political positions. The former Prime Minister, Hugh Shearer, exemplifies this new mobility.** A dark-skinned man, he is not as well educated as many political leaders, and began his political career as a staff member of the Bustamante Industrial Trade Union newspaper. He is able, however, to convey the impression of a respectable, middle-class leader who mingles comfortably with diplomats and members of the Jamaican elite. Thus, political power, especially at the national level, has become a means by which upwardly mobile persons can legitimate their prestige to other members of the society; the esteem which they command stems not only from their middle-class manners, speech patterns, and life styles, but also from the power and prestige inherent in the offices they hold.

---

* Many of the newly-created government service jobs, especially at the local level, are awarded primarily on the basis of educational qualification, and not through political connections.

** Sir Alexander Bustamante has retired from political life, and Hugh Shearer, former president of the Bustamante Industrial Trade Union, is now head of the Labour Party. Norman Manley died in 1969, and his son, Michael, is presently the Prime Minister of Jamaica. The former head of the National Workers' Union, Michael Manley is a light-skinned man who projects an image similar to his father's—that of a thoughtful and intelligent man.

POLITICAL ORGANIZATION IN COCO HILL *

There are two elected government officials for the area which includes Coco Hill: the Parish Councillor, who serves in the St. Ann
Parish Council,** and the Member of Parliament, who serves in the
national House of Representatives. How is the political organization
behind these men structured at the local level? What opportunities do
the political parties provide for social mobility, either toward positions
of leadership or toward other types of benefits?

Political Positions in the Community

There are four local branches of national political organizations
in Coco Hill: the Coco Hill PNP, formed in 1951, meets monthly in the
shop of a successful entrepreneur; the Coolside PNP branch, formed
in 1965, meets infrequently in the shop of its secretary; Cane Road's
JLP branch, formed in 1952, meets monthly in its chairman's shop;
and the Coco Hill "Victorious" JLP branch, formed in 1967, meets
weekly at a member's shop. There are four official positions in each of
the branches: chairman, vice-chairman, secretary, and treasurer; the
most important officer in each case is the chairman. Committees are
often formed to supervise branch activities, thus creating more official
positions.

To what extent is leadership in these branches open? My research
reveals that leadership in the party branches is based on high status in
the community, so that position in the parties is not an independent
source of prestige. However, there is one local exception to this general
trend, which suggests that opportunity for advancement through local
official leadership positions in political parties is not completely
blocked.

The leaders of the parties in Coco Hill—usually men—tend to be
among the more successful individuals in the village. They are big
farmers, entrepreneurs, or white-collar workers, and are leaders in
local branches of other nation-wide associations. For example, the head
of the Coco Hill PNP branch, Mr. Clarke, is a 55-year-old black man
who owns 25 acres of land. He inherited this land from his father, who

* In my discussion of politics in Coco Hill in this and the following chapter,
the ethnographic present is 1968–69, when the JLP was in power nationally.

** The St. Ann Parish Council, one of 12 on the island, supervises poor relief,
sanitation, street cleaning, maintenance of parochial roads, garbage collection,
water supply, fire protection, public health, parks, and markets. It is funded
through special rates and taxes collected by the central government, and direct
grants from the central government.

was a farmer, carpenter, elder at the Methodist Church, and past president of the Jamaica Agricultural Society. Mr. Clarke serves as secretary of the Jamaica Agricultural Society, treasurer of the Credit Union, and is an officer in the Methodist Church. His wife is the librarian at the local branch library, an officer in the Credit Union, and was, until three years ago, the vice-chairman of the PNP branch. The Clarkes' three children have become, respectively, a teacher, secretary, and bank clerk. Two of Mr. Clarke's brothers live in Coco Hill and they too inherited 25 acres of land from their father. One is an elder at a local church and secretary of the All-Island Banana Growers' Association. The other is a Justice of the Peace and heads the local branch of the All-Island Banana Growers' Association and the People's Cooperative Bank. Two other brothers live in nearby towns; one runs a trucking business, the other heads a government agency in the parish capital. Similarly, the treasurer of the Coco Hill PNP branch, a 50-year-old black man who owns over 15 acres of land, is an elder at the Baptist Tabernacle Church, and both he and his wife are officers in the local agricultural society; their daughter attends secondary school.

In contrast, the head of the Coco Hill JLP branch is an unsuccessful small farmer, and he has experienced difficulty as a leader. A 57-year-old black man, Mr. Munroe comes from a family respected by the community. His father was a District Constable and one of his brothers is a successful shopkeeper. After he left school, Mr. Munroe was apprenticed to a tailor but, he explains, he was left-handed and since the tailor insisted that he use his right hand, he never could "get the hang of it." Instead, he took up farming on two acres of his father's land, and in the mid-1940's went to the United States on contract as a farm worker. He saved enough money to buy on his return four acres of land and five cows. However, disease struck all of his cows and he was forced to sell some of his land to meet expenses, and even to work out as a cane cutter on a nearby sugar estate. His economic failure occasioned a change in church allegiance; he left the Seventh Day Adventist Church and joined the Pentecostal Church: "Seeing the poor condition and can't work on Saturday, to raise the children and sometime you have a thing to sell. It was hard so I switch over. Most of them in the Adventist is big people." Mr. Munroe became a deacon at the Pentecostal Church—a post he no longer holds—and vice-chairman of the Cane Road JLP. In 1967, "seeing as there was hardly any Labourite in Coco Hill, I decided to start a branch. The Councillor ask me to start one. So I get around to the people and show them the good that Mr. Bustamante do. I make a house-to-house campaign, nobody pay me. Just jump around and get a place. We start with 20 members and we have 75 now." Despite Mr. Munroe's leadership position in the JLP branch, his occupation, land holdings, income, and life style define him as a person of low rank in the district. He cannot afford to buy "respectable" new clothes, and the poor, two-room, government-built "owner-occupied" house in which he lives with his wife and seven children is a symbol of his low status, since only the poorest in the community can qualify for one of these houses. Thus far, none of his children has been successful in life; the four eldest are in Kingston, "just ordinary work, not in any job," and one daughter attends the JSC classes at the Anglican Church. To earn cash he often works out on the road or hires his labor to other farmers in the area. He finds these jobs humiliating and told me that he works for big farmers because they are his friends. He frequently complains about his poverty and regrets that he cannot "live the life them expect of a leader. The people are looking to me to live up to a certain principle. I can't be too ragged on the street because I am a leader."

It is because of Mr. Munroe's low status in Coco Hill that his position in the Labour Party branch is especially important to him. Now that he no longer holds an office at the church it is his one claim to prestige in the community. He is anxious to get benefits for the members of the branch and devotes a lot of time to party business or merely helping members of the group in times of need. For example, he spent one Sunday collecting money from villagers of both parties to hire a car for a very poor member of the group who was seriously ill and had to be transported to the hospital. He is sensitive to slights from the Parish Councillor or other executive officers of the JLP, who tend to condescend to him. The Parish Councillor, in particular, wants to replace him with a more prosperous and "progressive" leader who understands the workings of parish politics better and does not constantly agitate for benefits for his own branch. The Parish Councillor, a 50-year-old black man who owns a successful business in a major town in the parish, has been grooming Mr. Cooper, a 27-year-old Coco Hill black man, for the post. Mr. Cooper has a skilled job with a bauxite company, is an officer in the Methodist Church, and owns about seven acres of land. He seldom attends the branch meetings; when he comes it is in a car with the Parish Councillor and other important JLP leaders. The Councillor feels that Mr. Cooper would not create as much trouble for him as Mr. Munroe does and this is probably true. Mr. Cooper is more secure in his status in the community than Mr. Munroe and would not feel the need to legitimate his rank, either to himself or to members of the local branch, by proving that he could secure benefits for group members. It would be more important to him to win the esteem of the parish-wide executives—

among them, the Parish Councillor—and he would be less likely to question the decisions of the Councillor.

These examples indicate that formal leadership posts in the local party branches can enhance a person's prestige in the village to some extent since leaders distribute benefits to members and act as middlemen between the villagers and elected officials. However, their prestige stems primarily from their occupation, land holdings, income, and life style; official position in the party branches tends to reinforce this status. Thus, Mr. Munroe is respected by members of the branch and other wage laborers and unsuccessful small farmers because he is a local party chairman. However, he is not considered an equal by big farmers, successful small farmers, or white-collar workers in Coco Hill.

Local party leaders derive little prestige or influence outside their communities from their political roles. One reason is that unless they are white-collar workers, they are defined as members of the society's lower class, and thus do not command deference from parish officials. Another is that their political base is too limited to enable them to demand benefits for their members. Each electoral division has many local party branches: for example, Coco Hill's Member of Parliament is responsible for about 25 branches, and the Parish Councillor for about eight. The power base of each local leader is very small, and the leaders are forced to compete with each other for political rewards. If a leader delivers votes to the politicians, he may receive benefits to distribute to his members; if not, he may be passed by. The Member of Parliament or Parish Councillor decides to which areas he will distribute benefits, and the branch chairmen can exert little pressure to change these decisions. The local leaders know that many factors influence the distribution of political rewards. For example, the Coco Hill PNP receives little help from the national and parish-wide political organizations, because Coco Hill is a solid PNP area, and the PNP executives feel there is no need for them to spend time there. Similarly, Mr. Munroe, although responsible for building up the Labour vote in Coco Hill to some extent, is aware that he wields no real power. This became clear during a dispute he had with the Parish Councillor. In trying to get a new public water tank for Coco Hill, Mr. Munroe finally tired of the Councillor's inaction on the issue and, on his own initiative, had the old tank's pollution level measured. He also rose at a parish-wide JLP executive meeting and accused the Councillor of neglecting his constituents, thereby violating the approved channels for expressing political demands and embarrassing the Councillor. The Councillor then came to Coco Hill for a private talk with Mr. Munroe. He denounced Mr. Munroe for his action and threatened to withhold future benefits from the branch. As a response Mr. Munroe told others that he would close down the group, stop working for the Councillor, and support another man in the coming election. However, in a later confrontation with the Councillor at an open meeting in Coco Hill, Mr. Munroe assumed a respectful and servile posture. He realized that he could easily be deposed, because if he angered the Councillor his group might get no benefits at all, and the members would not support his bellicose actions if he could offer them no concrete promises of aid.

Opportunities for advancement in the national and parish political hierarchy are also limited for local leaders. Candidates for the House of Representatives are chosen by the National Executive Committees of the parties and local leaders stand no chance of being selected for this post. Some may run for Parish Council, but even this post is out of reach for most local leaders. It is costly to run for the Parish Council and only very successful merchants, professionals, or farmers can afford a political campaign. In addition, holding office is time-consuming and Councillors are not paid for their services. The only man from Coco Hill who ever served on the Parish Council owned over 300 acres of land and employed six men on a regular basis at the time he ran for office.

Patronage

For the vast majority in Coco Hill, politics is a matter of getting help in the form of material assistance from one of the parties, rather than holding official positions in party branches. Ideological issues are of minimal concern or significance. In turn, the amount of patronage awarded to party supporters in the community is a reflection of the balance of power in the parish and nation. In Coco Hill one party does not monopolize all the benefits to be distributed and the exercise of patronage by both parties is a factor in minimizing political conflict.

The Member of Parliament allots a number of benefits to his supporters. Among these are contract cards which enable holders to work on farms in the United States for several months of the year under an agreement between the Jamaican government and American companies or individuals, employment as laborers on main roads, poor-relief food, repairs for houses, and poll watching jobs on Election Day. The Parish Councillor is in charge of such benefits as parochial road work, installation of electric lights, distribution of government-subsidized homes, and government-built latrines.

However, the party affiliations of elected officials and the party composition of the bodies in which they serve affect the amount of patronage they can distribute. During my stay in the community, the

Member of Parliament for the area which included Coco Hill belonged to the PNP, the official Opposition party at the national level, and the Parish Councillor, who belonged to the JLP, served on a PNP-dominated Parish Council. Although the Member of Parliament had benefits to distribute, he would have had more if he had belonged to the Labour Party, that is, the party in power nationally. The Parish Councillor, a member of the parish Opposition, received many benefits for his supporters directly through Ministers in the national government. The Parish Council is dependent for its revenue on the national government; part of this money is divided equally among all the Councillors, and part is reserved for Councillors belonging to the majority party in the Council. Thus, a former Parish Councillor for Coco Hill who was elected as an Independent explained that he switched to the PNP to receive extra funds, even though the PNP put up a candidate to run against him and the JLP did not:

> The majority party always gets more things than the lesser party. When money come from the imperial government, the Council keep one-third for emergency and if you are a member of that party you get a preference or else you only get what is allotted to you twice a year.

The PNP was in power nationally at the time that he served in the PNP-dominated St. Ann Council and therefore it received a great deal of support from the central government.

When I was in Coco Hill, the PNP also dominated the St. Ann Council, but it was then the Opposition party nationally, and the Council received very little aid from Kingston. In fact, at one of the meetings I attended, a request for £55,000 to be spent on road repairs was answered with a contribution of £500 by the Minister of Local Government.* However, as a member of the Labour Party, the Parish Councillor for Coco Hill was able to appeal to the Minister of Local Government and other Cabinet Ministers, and to secure from them money to repair several roads, to install a number of lights, and to supply one section with water and electricity. Thus, although the PNP Councillors received a larger share of the Parish Council pie, that pie was considerably smaller in the St. Ann Council than in the councils dominated by the Labour Party, and Labourites in the St. Ann Council got additional funds for their constituents through Cabinet Ministers.

---

* After a number of PNP Councillors burst into sarcastic laughter, a debate ensued over what to do about the insult. The PNP Councillors voted to return the money to the Minister and argued that £500 was an insult. The JLP Councillors disagreed. They knew that they would receive help anyway from the Minister of Local Government and, as is the case with every issue that arises in the Council meetings, took a stand opposite to that of the PNP.

Both the Parish Councillor and the Member of Parliament spend money with political ends in mind; in general, they reward those areas which have supported them well and "punish" those areas where votes have slipped off in recent years. Other considerations may affect this pattern. A Parish Councillor or Member of Parliament who wishes to gain support in a strong Opposition area may pour money into that section to woo new supporters and, in some cases, he may neglect areas in which he is traditionally strong. For example, the Labour Party pours aid into the upper sections of Coco Hill, while the PNP has been trying to build up its strength in the Cane Road district. Other, more personal interests are also involved. For example, the Parish Councillor for Coco Hill bought 20 acres of land in one part of the community. Although voting records reveal that the area is equally divided between PNP and Labour support, he supplied the area with electricity and piped water (a luxury unknown to the other sections), had the road paved, and was trying to convince the central government to build a school there.

Meetings of the Local Branches

Actual operations of the political system on the local level may be observed at branch meetings of political parties in the village. Officers in the branches stress the benefits they can distribute to their supporters. It is mainly for the sake of these benefits that branch chairmen are active at election time in canvassing and transporting known supporters to the polls. If the candidate from his party wins, the chairman will have more patronage to distribute, and this enhances his status with group members. Attendance at meetings and the type of people who attend reflect the chairman's ability to distribute patronage to loyal supporters.

Meetings of the Coco Hill PNP branch are very poorly attended. Although it has 224 members, there are rarely more than 15 present, and only about 10 people show up regularly. In fact, at one meeting the future of the branch was in jeopardy since only seven persons were listed as dues-paying members. Low attendance at the meetings is a frequent topic of discussion and one member told me: "We have over 200 members but they don't attend. I try to encourage the member but they say they can't make it. They know we are a strong group here. When the PNP was in power, you couldn't get a seat but every meeting now we are fewer and fewer." The chairman continually tells the members "not to weary although we are few" and to keep up the "comrade" * spirit.

* PNP members refer to one another as "comrade"; JLP members refer to each other as "brother." The PNP symbol is the broom; the JLP symbol the bell.

Initially I was struck by the group's rather lethargic leadership and attributed the failure of the group to this factor. However, there are many capable and dynamic PNP supporters in the community and the same officials who appear passive at political meetings can be fired with enthusiasm at other association meetings. Rather, the key factor is that the branch cannot effectively help its members. The PNP controls the distribution of contract cards, gives out road work to its members, distributes some poor-relief food, and provides a few members with employment as poll watchers on Election Day, but since the Parish Councillor is a Labourite and the PNP Member of Parliament's benefits are limited because he belongs to the Opposition party in the House of Representatives, the PNP cannot help its members get many of the benefits they want and need. These include government-subsidized houses, catchment tank loans, and jobs on government projects. Furthermore, parish and national officials are sure of support in Coco Hill and are more concerned with earning gratitude—and votes—in areas where the party is weak.

If there are few benefits for PNP supporters, why do the 10 members continue to attend the meetings month after month? The "regulars" at the PNP meetings tend to be respected persons in the community, that is, big farmers and entrepreneurs, white-collar workers, and more successful small independent farmers. The men come regularly because affiliation with the branch and official position within it are supplementary sources of prestige, as they are in other voluntary associations in the village such as the Jamaica Agricultural Society and the All-Island Banana Growers' Association. To occupy an official position in one of these groups, or merely to attend as a member and have an equal voice in decisions and discussions with those in formal leadership posts, confirms one's elite status in the community. The same men and women generally hold offices in all of the groups, and for this reason the meetings take on a cliquish air. There is a relatively large turnout only when a concrete benefit may be gained by attending. The meetings, for example, at which the agricultural officer distributes forms for fertilizer subsidies are well attended. At these meetings, the nonregulars leave as soon as they receive their forms; they do not participate in the discussions and seem to feel uncomfortable and out of place.

Discussions at the PNP meetings are influenced by the type of people attending and generally center around problems of formal organization and fund raising. Occasionally a poor member attends to ask if he can get a new government home or pit latrine. The chairman then explains that he can only help to get a home repaired and that the Parish Councillor controls the distribution of government-subsidized homes and pit latrines. At monthly meetings that I attended, a major

debate revolved around the fact that the treasurer never attended the
meetings. The treasurer was on bad terms with a big farmer who
attended regularly and who usually dominated the proceedings. The
latter insisted that the treasurer should be deposed (and implied that
he be the replacement). Since the chairman controlled decisions of
this nature, and was a close friend of the treasurer, the solution at each
meeting was to send an "ultimatum" to the treasurer and to give him
one last chance; at the time I left Coco Hill he was still an officer
although he had not attended one meeting. Another major topic of
discussion was the formation of various committees, in particular, a
committee to organize a raffle to raise funds for the group. Many discussions were held to decide how committee members should be
selected, the wisdom of having a committee at all, the prizes to be
offered, and the price of tickets. A reading of the minutes of past
meetings revealed that the question of holding a raffle has continued
for two years. The last raffle took place in 1965 and so few tickets were
sold that the group actually lost money.

In contrast, the Labour Party branch in Coco Hill is a more
dynamic and active group. Formed in 1967, it has been carefully
nurtured by the St. Ann Labour Party as part of an attempt to gain
control of a PNP-dominated area. The group has 79 members, of whom
15 to 20 usually attend meetings. Unlike every other association and
party branch in the community, this group meets weekly—a tactic
devised by parish-wide executives who felt that if meetings were
scheduled every week, members would become more closely affiliated
with the party. In addition, Labour executives in the parish organization make frequent visits to the meetings.

Members who attend meetings do so in order to obtain some concrete benefit. Without exception they are the poorest people in the community, wage laborers who own under an acre of land, work out in the
most menial jobs, and live in the most humble dwellings. More than
half of those who attend regularly are elderly women; many who come
feel a sense of belonging to the group and look forward to seeing their
"fellow sufferers" assembled and being given a collective opportunity
to bemoan their fate. A description from my field notes of one typical
meeting illustrates these points:

> The JLP meets every Monday night in the shop at the top of the
> road. The room is long and narrow and dark since the sole lighting
> comes from the lamp which is perched atop the table. The chair-
> man stands behind the table and the secretary sits to the side.
> Members come in alone, one by one; the women sit on one side,
> the men on the other. As the members enter they say "good
> evening" to one another and quietly take their seats on the wooden
> benches. The chairman usually has difficulty lighting the lamp,

complains about the cost of fixing it, and utters, "it is hard, it is
hard" a number of times. The secretary is invariably late. She
comes in after 8:00 and the meeting can then formally begin. The
members stand up to sing "We Plow the Fields and Scatter," an
old hymn, and the chairman selects a "brother" to lead the group
in prayer. He then welcomes all to the meeting and the secretary
reads, somewhat falteringly, the minutes of the last meeting. The
chairman goes through the ritual of mentioning old business and
new business to be discussed but usually enters into a long speech
about his latest encounter with the Parish Councillor or other
important men in the parish-wide executive committee. He tells
the group what benefits to expect and how to agitate for their
demands since rarely do any members bring up old or new business
in this formal way. He tries to encourage members and tells them
the best way to go about making their demands known. These
ways change continually so that at one meeting they are told to
badger the Parish Councillor, to go to the parish capital on certain
days of the week to see him, and not to "give up the hope" while
two weeks later they are instructed to give their request to the
branch chairman and not to go to the Parish Councillor directly.
There is usually little discussion from the members; some make
their traditional plea and complaint, asking when the road will
be cut or when the Councillor will come to look at their poor shack.
Often the speeches of the chairman are interrupted by wry comments from the members about the possibility of getting help, such
as "a promise is only comfort for a fool" or "them is too miserable."
Nonetheless, they continue to come week after week with their
complaints and faith in the Labour Party. Occasionally a member
falls asleep during the proceedings and most are anxious to get
home to bed. However, there is a certain group solidarity at these
meetings, a common feeling of suffering between the officials—
also poor—and the members. The meetings usually adjourn at
about 9:15; the men and women and sleepy children file out in
groups and wearily head home.

The dominant theme at all of the meetings is the benefits to be received. For example, the chairman opened one meeting in this way:

> We thank God for keeping us through the past week and six
> months past and gone. The most we can have is the good Saviour
> to lead us. This is a time when we can't do it for ourself. Who can
> tell us tonight is not the last chance in our life? Some people say
> we are here only to talk foolishness. Our intention is not for that
> but to live for Him alone. We gather here tonight to learn more
> about our country. We want things to come forward, whether to
> help ourself. We pray that our visitor [the Parish Councillor]
> catch up and advise our attention tonight. As you know, in a
> church if you only hear the deacon all night long you wonder

what become of the parson. I want to feel that they are on the way coming. I am going to say to him, what about the £100 for Mr. Turner street. If Brother Turner get sick we won't be able to visit him. We are going to put it to him. Use the £100 and we will clean up the street. Be a man tonight. Speak up. Another point again. When I speak about the toilet, make him know how it bad, let him know how it stay. We know that this branch started some time ago. We want it to keep movin' on. Those who want to still receive, we'll fight the good old fight. Who don't receive, will receive something.

At every meeting I attended, the members complained about the toilet or new house they wanted or the road that needed repair and the chairman advised them of the best way to proceed. It was made clear that the only way to get these benefits was to be a known Labourite, to get a card from the JLP branch, and then to keep trying to get what was needed. When the Parish Councillor came to meetings he cited what he had done for the district, for example, the amount of money spent on various roads or the number of street lights installed. He urged them to continue in their support:

I want to promise you that all Labourites will hear my voice. You young boys and girls and old men I am giving you the warning. Work for your section. People in my division come to me and I never refuse one . . . . You have to work through the branch and I will get to know you. I'll do the best for the people that I am satisfied with and when I'm not sure I'll ask the chairman or the secretary.

The people who attend the meetings week after week have great patience. Some have been coming for two years merely to get a road paved through to their home. They are continually promised by the Councillor that the road will be paved, for example, and they wait for the day when he will actually fulfill his promise.

CONCLUSION

The local branches of the national parties are designed to consolidate rural support by building strong local organizations, that is, by recruiting new members and retaining old ones through the promises of concrete benefits, and making sure that these members vote on Election Day. The parties do not offer the villagers the opportunity to occupy prestigious and influential political roles in the society and their major function is the distribution of patronage to supporters. The following chapter discusses some consequences of the limited role political parties play in the community.

VIII

Politics and
Interpersonal Relations

Since politics involves various types of competitive struggles, it might be expected that politics, as well as competition for educational advancement, is an important source of interpersonal conflict in Coco Hill. However, my field investigations reveal that politics is rarely a basis for disputes within the community.

ATTITUDES TOWARD THE GOVERNMENT
AND POLITICAL PARTIES

To the villagers of Coco Hill, the Jamaican government appears to help only the "haves" and the "bigger men," and to neglect "we the poor people."

Most of Coco Hill's residents feel that although there have been many significant improvements in the past 20 years, notably increased educational opportunities, there is also much to complain of—for example, prices have risen, particularly since devaluation of the pound in 1967, and conversion to the decimal system in 1969. Store-bought items continue to rise in cost, but the prices that farmers receive for crops have not risen and have, in some cases, fallen. Thus, when I asked about the effects of independence, villagers told me:

Since independence? Is hard for me to see it. I can't see any difference. It appears to me it worse today. Everything is so expensive and you can't get anything to do.

Things are much dearer. This government giving we hell. Definitely worse. The economic standard has deteriorated. You may run a little more but inflation of prices, no comparison.

Independence mash we up a lot. The things them are rather harder to get and it is dearer. Some are in no position to carry on ourself or run our situation.

They blame the current state of affairs on the ineffectiveness or, more commonly, the bad intentions of the central government. Many in the village complain, for example, that "the Jamaican government unfair. Don't see that every man and woman get a job. If you thief they fine you, when you dead they come to see you. But not when you alive. If the government would see to it that people could get something to do. . . ." Or, "If the person die fe [for] hungry, the government pay doctor to find out what kill you. That's the only time the government come." The two persons quoted are loyal Labour Party supporters— not only PNPs are frustrated by the government's programs.

Dissatisfaction with the government's programs is heightened by the gap between the new political elites' claims that they are equalizing chances for success and the fact of continued inequalities in Jamaican society. The villagers of Coco Hill want benefits from the government which will alter their own or their children's occupational status. Many feel that the government willfully denies aid to poor villagers simply because they are poor, and that it has unlimited funds which it could use to help people in areas like Coco Hill, if it had the desire. They sense that the government helps the "bigger shot":

Government look after those who have something doing already. Not the poorer. After the civil servant strike for pay and they raise the prices but they not looking on those people who work in the fields or without jobs. Robber man! [Labour Party supporter]

Is much better for the bigger fish but we the smaller are suffering. It will be worse in the future if the government doesn't help the poor one. Can hardly buy sugar. You do the farming, no good land can you get and them say they pay for peas and corn and when you reap there is no price for it. And they not helping you with the money to farm. They give you no help. Is just wrong. The island all right for the rich man and the fool. But the poor man, is easier to die than to live. The fool don't want no uplifting and the rich don't need it. [PNP supporter]

Nobody give me nuthin'. We don't get nuthin'. Only the bigger shot get help. [Labour Party supporter]

Many feel that if the United States would help Jamaica, these in-equities might become less marked. Many also stated to me that Jamaica was better off as a British colony, and some said that "if America come to take over Jamaica, thing would be better. You wouldn't find so many people out of a job. That's why Jamaica so mash up. Poverty every day." Thus, the colonial legacy lingers on in Coco Hill. Many reminders of British rule remain; for example, many still refer to the government as the "imperial government," pictures of Queen Elizabeth II hang on the walls of many homes, and at a meeting of the agricultural society the president announced the singing of the national anthem by saying, "Let's stand and sing the Queen." However, the villagers now count on the United States—Jamaica's new "colonial power"—to deliver them from poverty.

Although most villagers are loyal to one party or the other, and election statistics reveal that the villagers have turned out at the polls in increasing numbers since 1944, most feel that neither party offers meaningful benefits, and claim that "the PNP and JLP would no different, for the upper sets get and the poorer class suffer." One PNP supporter, a black man who farms five acres of land, told me:

> Regardless of which in power, I has to work very hard so I don't interested in one or the other. When I was a lad I buy tobacco for my old lady to sell and there was this man, he was trying to go to the House for this area and there is no time when he meets us on the road when he doesn't take us up in his car. And, from the time when him win the elections, him go by in car and don't see you. These are the type of people we has to deal with. None of them is no good. I am a PNP but I remember the time when the PNP was in power. Manley was making a plan where he was helping the smaller man, tanks and cowshed and thing. When I apply for a tank they tell me my land too small for a tank. I had a half acre. Some of them get tank and have river behind their home! The man who afford it, get it, the man who need it, don't.

The nature of certain government loans to farmers and the require-ments to qualify for them discriminate against poor farmers. Loans for building catchment tanks and for pasture improvement, for example, are only partial loans. To qualify for such a loan a farmer must prove that he can provide the remaining cash needed and that he has a cer-tain amount of land to put up as collateral. Thus, while many villagers receive small food-crop and fertilizer subsidies, only the better-off receive "tank and cowshed" loans.

Some comments of the villagers regarding the parties were:

> The whole outfit, I don't think nothing about for no one help me. I has to work for myself. [Labour Party supporter]

Sometime you put in with one side and they hardly do anything to help you so you have to say both of them carry on same way. People talk about them party. Say this one is better. Me just leave them. Me no see no progress with the parties. Young people can't get work, sit down and study wicked things, hold people up in the street. Is terrible. [PNP supporter]

It seems to me that neither party not doing anything. They come in at election time and want your vote and promise you anything. I change over to the PNP, maybe get a little get out. [PNP supporter]

You have to work for yourself anyway. None of them help you. No sir. None of them help you. Even want a shilling and none of them help me. If you Labour you have to work for yourself, if you PNP you have to work for yourself. [Labour Party supporter]

A heavy-equipment operator for one of the bauxite companies—a "stranger" who attended secondary school in Kingston for two years—identifies with the PNP but criticized both parties:

Both of them same thing. Take for instance, Michael Manley come down to the mine and say we are supposed to get food if you work four hours overtime and he got through with that the last contract and there was about 500 of us workers at the meeting. He say, "OK boys, we got overtime food" and the boys go "yeah, yeah" and nobody asks what kind of food and it was aerated [soda] water and biscuits and sardine. And we are supposed to be handling 50- to a 1000-ton machines! The people are illiterate. Both of them same thing. Two cousins.* If one party in power, look for gross discrimination to the other. No difference.

Thus, most villagers feel that there is little difference between the parties. Jamaican newspapers and radio give the impression that conflict between members of the two political parties is common, but in fact, such conflict rarely arises in Coco Hill.

POLITICS AND INTERPERSONAL DISPUTES

Although there is some political conflict and some spontaneous fighting over politics in Coco Hill, there are several reasons why politics provides neither the basis for most local disputes nor the means through which they are expressed. First, one party does not monopolize the available patronage. Second, most of the benefits distributed by the parties are considered unappealing by the majority in the village. Third, party affiliation crosscuts such significant social ties as kinship, resi-

* Alexander Bustamante and Norman Manley were first cousins.

dence, and church and association membership, and does not correlate
with status group divisions.

Attitudes Toward Benefits

The benefits distributed by the political parties to their supporters
in the village are not highly valued by most in the community. A person
must not only prove extreme poverty to qualify for them, but one of the
most readily available benefits, road work, is regarded as a very low-
status pursuit. The majority of Coco Hill residents feel that neither
party provides them with the kind of benefits which they consider
significant, that is, those which would alter their own or their children's
occupational status. For example, many complained that "what
Coco Hill needs is a place where there is a factory so young boys and
women could help themselves." * Others desired increased opportunities
to attend secondary school or to go abroad to do nonagricultural work.

One PNP supporter told me, "In Coco Hill, don't get none [help]
from one [party] or the other. We don't get no help. Only give out food
at election time, poorhouse food. Only get them free food and shoe at
election time and crop time them get work and weedin' the road." Most
small farmers and certainly big farmers, entrepreneurs, and white-collar
workers are anxious to dissociate themselves from the poorest members
of the community and to establish their own superior status. They are
therefore reluctant to accept jobs or help which might define them as
persons of low rank, and do not feel victimized when such supposed
benefits are not made available to them. Most young men do not want
the contract cards distributed by the PNP; they view agricultural labor
as degrading even when it is done abroad. Big farmers and
entrepreneurs, as well as most small farmers, prefer to avoid low-status
tasks such as Christmas work.** Nor do they desire government-
subsidized houses, which, although new, indicate the owner's low
status, since a person must be very poor to qualify for such housing.

However, some villagers would like to receive these benefits,
and attend party meetings regularly in order to do so. Who are they

* Although both men and women complained about the types of employment available, it was primarily women who expressed an interest in bringing a
factory to Coco Hill. Women are cash earners in over 50 per cent of the families in
the village. However, the traditional occupations for farmers' wives—higglering
and cultivating—are relatively low-status occupations and yield a low cash income.
On the other hand, factory work is salaried and relatively well-paid in comparison
to agricultural, domestic, or market work.

** At Christmas time, both parties give out work on the roads. Men weed and
women sweep. This work usually lasts for a week or two and is referred to as
Christmas work.

and why do they want political favors? In general, they are wage laborers and unsuccessful small farmers—the poorest people in Coco Hill. They want these benefits because there are few other opportunities available to them to earn cash; they have little if any land, and lack the skills necessary to follow nonagricultural occupations, or the capital to invest in small-scale businesses. Their major source of cash is working out for others in the community in menial capacities. Thus, the benefits they receive from political parties represent an important part of their income, and to obtain some of the benefits, such as the government houses and free food, does not require any work. Work on the roads or farm labor abroad is deemed more desirable than local farm work because supervisors on road crews are frequently men from outside the community and, of course, farm labor abroad is done for Americans. Thus, laborers do not have to subordinate themselves to those tied to them by kinship, residence, or church membership. Furthermore, since their occupation, land holdings, life style, and income indicate their low status in the village, they do not lose prestige by accepting political favors. The favors provide an acceptable means to improve income and living conditions.

When wage laborers and unsuccessful small farmers do not receive available help or jobs they rarely quarrel with persons of similar status in the opposition party who do receive these benefits, as they might in cases where educational opportunities are involved; the benefits are not symbols of prestige, so those who have succeeded in obtaining them are not envied. Rather, they are hostile towards those persons of high status charged with distributing the benefits. These persons are believed to dispense favors to their friends and are envied because they follow desired occupations and life styles and are able to send their children to secondary school. In most social situations these persons receive deference from the less successful villagers, and resentment is rarely expressed openly. Hostility towards their success finds expression through such means as obeah accusations or bitter remarks in conversations with status equals.

Since wage laborers and unsuccessful small farmers appreciate help from the parties they are more likely than white-collar workers, big farmers and entrepreneurs, or successful small farmers to alter their political allegiance and to attend party meetings regularly. Thus, many who regularly attended Labour Party meetings in Coco Hill had recently switched to the JLP. In the words of the chairman, they did so "'cause they are poor people, they need of help." Since the parish-wide JLP wants to strengthen its political base in Coco Hill, it distributes many benefits to loyal party members there, while the PNP has recently tried to win support in Cane Road by giving members there a number of benefits; the PNP Member of Parliament has even made several tours of the area and once took a sick man, a Labourite, to the hospital in his own car.

Even villagers of low status, however, do not often change their political allegiance to get help. Although politics is largely a matter of economic assistance, party loyalty has emotional overtones for some villagers. Moreover, if one's relatives and neighbors are strong supporters of one party, an individual hesitates to transfer his allegiance to the other party, even if he may get material benefits in the process. Those most likely to alter their political allegiance are unsuccessful small farmers or wage laborers who are also downwardly mobile or "strangers." Downwardly mobile persons have already suffered a loss of esteem in the village and are willing to risk the disdain of their kin and fellows and use whatever benefits they receive to try to re-establish their old position; "strangers" have few, if any, relatives in the village to bring subtle pressures to bear on them to maintain old political ties.

Crosscutting Ties

People prefer that their close friends and kin identify with the political party they themselves support, but differing political orientations of friends or relations rarely lead to disputes. If disputes between them do arise, politics is seldom mentioned. Politics is not important enough to risk severing close social bonds for, or to become an issue in ongoing quarrels.

For example, in the national society, civil servants are generally identified with the PNP. This trend is less marked in Coco Hill; although a majority of the white-collar workers in the village do belong to the PNP, many teachers, bauxite employees, prison warders, as well as the Post Mistress, a social-welfare worker, and two nurses, affiliate with the Labour Party. Among the white-collar workers of Coco Hill, common life style, status aspirations, attendance at certain churches, and leadership in associations are powerful bonds which override the importance of party affiliation. For example, the fact that the Post Mistress is a Labourite is not important to other white-collar workers in the village who are eager to gain her favor because of her prestigious position and the fact that her husband has an important job with one of the bauxite companies.

Following the general pattern of disputes in the village, quarrels between white-collar workers generally revolve around insults, and because politics is not a sensitive area in terms of defining status, it is rarely an issue. For example, a teacher in the village, Mrs. Barrett, is a

PNP supporter who has had a long-standing quarrel with Mrs. Winter, a nurse and Labourite. The dispute first arose when the nurse, then Miss Hines, did not invite Mrs. Barrett to her wedding: Miss Hines was venting some of the resentment and envy that had accumulated over the years as a result of what she considered Mrs. Barrett's continual and unwarranted haughtiness and assertion of superiority. The two women, "strangers" to Coco Hill, moved to the community about 10 years ago. They were then both unmarried and lived in rented rooms. They were close friends, and often went to church together and spent hours chatting after work. Mrs. Barrett was the first to achieve her desired goals in life; six years ago she married a civil servant and they proceeded to build one of the most modern homes in the community. Miss Hines climbed more slowly to social success. She remained single and continued to live in rented rooms until the winter of 1968, when she married the head of one of the government agencies in the parish. Although late in marrying, she succeeded in "catching" a more prestigious mate than Mrs. Barrett, and she and her husband plan to move to a respectable middle-class housing estate on the north coast. By not inviting Mrs. Barrett to the wedding, she dealt a blow to the teacher's pride; several other white-collar workers in Coco Hill were invited, and the ceremony was held in an expensive north coast hotel. Mrs. Barrett was indignant; she felt that she, of all people, should have been invited, since she is a respected person in the village and she and Miss Hines had been good friends. In retaliation, she refused to speak to Miss Hines, spread malicious rumors about her, and tried in vain to dissuade their mutual friends from going to the wedding. However, she never resorted to party politics, despite the fact that Miss Hines, unlike many of her peers in Coco Hill, was a member of the JLP. It simply was not considered relevant to the personal conflict between Mrs. Barrett and her former friend.

Party loyalty is usually secondary to personal loyalty. For example, Mr. Jackson, an officer in the local PNP, and one of the most successful farmers in the village, was having an affair with the village social-welfare worker, known to be a dedicated Labourite. One day when I was interviewing Mr. Jackson, a prominent PNP politician was also visiting him. The politician complained that the social-welfare worker had illegally tampered with the ballot boxes in the last election. Mr. Jackson agreed quietly, but was obviously embarrassed by being caught between the two loyalties, one to his party and the other to his mistress. He ended the discussion by saying that she was a "tricky" woman, but a very good person.

It is true that many white-collar workers—particularly the better-educated ones with close kinship and friendship ties to white-collar workers elsewhere on the island—see their PNP affiliation as a bond which unites them with other respectable citizens. Even so, they generally do not stress their political preferences except among members of their own party, usually when they speak to friends and relatives who do not live in Coco Hill. Within the community their close friends are often Labourites and in this context they tend to "joke off the party business." In Coco Hill they identify first and foremost with those who share the same status aspirations, life styles, and occupations, whether they belong to the PNP or the JLP. Mrs. Barrett, for example, would participate in political discussions when members of her family, civil servants, and professionals in Kingston and larger towns came to visit; in these talks the JLP would be ridiculed, Labourites identified with the ignorant masses, and the leaders of the JLP denounced and compared unfavorably to the more intelligent PNP leaders, particularly Norman Manley and his son. However, in Coco Hill, many of Mrs. Barrett's friends are Labourites. She likes them because they are "respectable," live in a "decent way," and know how to "act right." She wishes to identify with the island's middle classes, and for this reason eagerly participates in political discussions with her kin. However, she also wishes to identify with the respectable people in the village where she lives and works, who are frequently Labourites. Thus, in the context of Coco Hill, party affiliation is not a meaningful index of social status and therefore plays a minimal role in local conversations and quarrels.

Another tie which crosscuts political affiliation is voluntary association membership. The absence of discussion of party politics at meetings of the Jamaica Agricultural Society, a group closely identified at the national level with the PNP, is notable. The island-wide heads of the JAS complain in the news media that they are victimized by the Labour government. They resent the fact that the Labour government has purposely minimized their powers and bypassed the association in developing agricultural policies and programs. However, political victimization of the JAS is not mentioned at any of the meetings in Coco Hill, even after a member of the branch reported on the annual meeting in Kingston which he had attended. This annual meeting had received headline treatment in the island newspaper because the Minister of Rural Land Development was shouted down by the crowd and prevented from completing a speech. The Minister had tried to tell the delegates that government agricultural programs were divorced from party politics, and then used the occasion to announce the appointment of members to the new Land Authorities. All those named were well-known Labour supporters.

At the meeting in Coco Hill the local delegate who had been at the meeting avoided speaking of this incident, because several JAS officers and regular members are Labourites. As the elite of Coco Hill's farmers, those active in the association meet regularly to discuss farming problems and to agitate for various benefits from the government. Although their requests are rarely granted, none of the local leaders ever publicly raised the possibility that this was due to the association's PNP identification, the reason continually suggested by parish and national association leaders. In private, a few of the officers complained about the Labour government, and intimated that low attendance at meetings was a result of certain Labour policies, such as the increase in membership dues, but at meetings these issues are not raised. Instead, politics is judiciously avoided and solidarity among the farmers maintained. The association continues to enhance their prestige locally and to give them the feeling that they have some say, however minimal, in government decisions.

Another reason the association leaders do not raise the issue of political victimization at meetings is that the policies of the government have not blocked their own opportunities to occupy positions of prestige and power. Nearly all of the officials realize that they stand no chance of being appointed to parish or national boards and therefore they do not complain if only important Labour Party officials are given these posts. Thus, the president of the JAS, a successful farmer and loyal PNP supporter, told me with enthusiasm about the new programs of the Land Authorities and did not complain that no PNP members were appointed to the St. Ann Authority. He hoped that the programs would help the farmers in Coco Hill, including himself, and he did not care whether it was the JLP or the PNP that sponsored them. He knew he would not be appointed to the parish posts and felt that whether the "big shots" were PNP or JLP would have little effect on policy decisions.

Since wide kinship networks extend throughout the village, most people have relatives, as well as friends and neighbors, church brethren, drinking mates, market companions, and fellow workers, in both parties. Marriage usually takes place within party lines, but husbands and wives may belong to different parties. For example, one of my informants is a loyal Labourite, as are her mother and brother, who live nearby; her mother faithfully attends the Labour Party meetings every Monday night. However, the woman's husband is an ardent PNP supporter, and an officer in the PNP-affiliated trade union at the lime factory, and many of her friends and neighbors are also PNPs. At the same time, her arch-enemy and next-door-neighbor, to whom she has not spoken for months, is a Labourite. It is not unusual for members of the same family to belong to different parties. For example, the three brothers of Mr. Munroe, the Labour chairman in Coco Hill, are PNP supporters. The owner of one of the village bakeries describes himself as "strictly PNP," while his brother, who operates a trucking service, is a "die-hard Labourite."

People know the affiliations of their neighbors and kin, and usually avoid political discussions with members of the opposing party, fearing that such conversations may lead to "fuss." While they assert that politically-inspired violence does not occur in Coco Hill, most of the villagers, like the white-collar workers who belong to the PNP, prefer to express their political opinions among those whom they know to be "of the same mind." Even at election time there is little "fuss." Although many villagers expressed partisan feelings during the election I witnessed—the Parish Council election of 1969—most maintained an outward air of cordiality and friendliness to those in both parties. There were no incidents in Coco Hill on Election Day, and the villagers had to satisfy their thirst for tales of violence and fraud with the details of an incident which occurred in Spanish Town, a large town near Kingston. It is true that men often discuss politics at great length in the rum shops, and fights occasionally develop around political issues, but even at the rum shops conversations generally focus on topics deemed more important by the men, such as agricultural programs, women, religion, and finding work.

Those villagers least willing to discuss politics generally belong to the minority party in their own particular neighborhood. For example, a 27-year-old black man who supports the PNP, lives in a predominantly Labour area, and has gone to the United States on a farm contract card given him by his PNP uncle for the past five years told me, "I don't preach the politics business. When voting day, I go to the polls and make my mark and just quit. I hold my opinion for myself for I know the party business is dangerous. If you for one side and the other for the other, is a very conscious matter, don't it." Similarly, a poor black woman, who lives in a PNP neighborhood but attends Labour Party meetings in the hope of getting a road paved through to her house in the bush said, "Each side giving against the other. A whole heap of people lose their lives for politics. Me go out and hear people talking, me draw one side, me no have people kill me for that."

Most people whom I interviewed were not interested in discussing politics and usually wanted to change the subject to one they cared more about and which more directly affected their lives and interests. For example, they spoke of the rise in prices, quarrels in progress, their church, and ambitions for their children. Nearly all affirmed that people pay relatively little attention to differences in party affiliation:

I so live with the people, PNP or JLP. We move together and drink together and they tell me their sorrow and I will tell them mine.

I know they are PNP and they know I am Labour. But we don't fight. We are just friend going through.

POLITICAL CLEAVAGE AND RESIDENCE

There is one division within the community—that of residential areas—which generally coincides with political party cleavages. This division is between Cane Road and Coco Hill. Cane Road refers to those sections of the community on or off the road to the north coast; Coco Hill refers to those sections higher up in the hills. Although some expressed the feeling that their section was "all mixed up," most in Cane Road felt that their area was predominantly Labour and most in Coco Hill felt that their area was mainly PNP. Election statistics reveal that this perception is generally accurate. Residents were even more adamant in insisting that those in the opposite section were affiliated with the other party. For example, a PNP member in Coco Hill said, "who vote for Labour is mostly in Cane Road," and a Labourite in Cane Road said, "now Coco Hill people, them love the PNP." However, politics rarely becomes a basis for disputes between residents of the two areas.

There are a number of factors which make each section distinct, but most of these are not clearly related to the particular party affiliation which predominates in each area. There is an ecological difference between the two. Cane Road is at a lower elevation than Coco Hill, has a warmer climate, and a different soil type. It is therefore more suitable than Coco Hill for growing such crops as bananas and cane. Bananas and cane, in contrast to the vegetable crops which predominate in Coco Hill, link farmers in Cane Road more closely to government agricultural policies and to world markets. Cane is sold to the sugar estate for processing and bananas are sold to the government *; vegetable crops are sold at internal markets on the island.

Geographical location is another important factor in the dual division. Since Cane Road is nearer to the north coast, it is closer to the sole surviving sugar estate in the parish. Until recently, many men from Cane Road used to cut cane on the estate during crop time. The development of local and national industries and the automation of certain tasks on the estate have meant that fewer men work there; when I was in the community only 15 men from Cane Road continued to cut cane during crop time. Although some men from Coco Hill also used to work at the estate, since Coco Hill is farther from the estate and closer to the new local industries, still fewer men continue to work at the

* In recent years, farmers have been adversely affected by low government subsidies and poor conditions on the world market for bananas.

estate now; only five men from Coco Hill cut cane there. In addition, Cane Road residents use markets and services in a north coast town, rather than going to the hill town which residents of Coco Hill are likely to frequent. Furthermore, unlike the sections which make up Coco Hill, Cane Road is not on the main road to Kingston. A bus to the north coast passes through Cane Road, but to get a bus to Kingston or Montego Bay, one must go to the Coco Hill crossroad. Most government services in the village, and nearly all of the churches, are in Coco Hill. The few local industries, as well as the prison, are also in Coco Hill.

There are many successful farmers, shopkeepers, and tradesmen in Cane Road, and among the bulk of the village's population, that is, wage laborers and small farmers, there do not appear to be any differences between residents of Cane Road and Coco Hill in types of homes, number of children sent to secondary school, or rate of church membership. However, most white-collar workers have settled in Coco Hill; only seven white-collar workers live in Cane Road as opposed to about 65 in Coco Hill. Due to the expansion of government services, the rise of industry in the parish, the founding of the prison, and the expansion of the school, white-collar workers began to come to the community in increasing numbers from the 1950's on. They settled in Coco Hill rather than in Cane Road because Coco Hill was on the main road, had electricity, and was near other government services. The fact that the vast majority live in Coco Hill means that there are more modern homes, more private catchment tanks, and more people who can afford to send their children to secondary school in this section than in Cane Road. Thus residents of Cane Road feel somewhat resentfully that those in Coco Hill are more successful:

> Some people in Coco Hill get on better. Some farm and them get employment at bauxite and improve themself better. It looks to me like people in Coco Hill getting through better than we. You see, according to how you see the buildings going on, you can see that they are doing better than we. Some of them have good jobs, their children do better than we . . .

> People in Coco Hill kind of more wealthier. Them can help themselves. Have a few wealthy down here but most is poor.

This resentment is sometimes linked to the political identification of Coco Hill residents since one party, different from their own, predominates there. But this feeling is directed primarily at the good fortune of people in Coco Hill; politics is relevant only as a characteristic associated with their success. Conversely, white-collar workers in Coco Hill tended to express contempt for those in Cane Road; since most are "strangers" they do not have relatives in that section and few persons of their status live there. They told me that they would not want to live in Cane Road because people there are "uncultured . . . they would never get married . . . carry on in all sorts of ways . . . don't know how to live right . . . are too out of order." Those white-collar workers who support the PNP often linked this contempt to politics. They said that the people in Cane Road who favor the JLP need the government's help because they work at the sugar estate and hire out their labor. It should be noted that this disdain is directed primarily against the need for help, not against the Labour Party itself.

Not everyone in Coco Hill, however, perceives status differences between residents of the two sections. For example, most small farmers, big farmers and entrepreneurs, and wage laborers who live in Coco Hill and have relatives in Cane Road—as most do—did not express a preference for living in Coco Hill. Their attitude is illustrated by the result of the census of Percy Road I took at the beginning of my stay there. One of the questions I asked was, "Is there any section of the community which you would prefer to live in? Prefer not to live in? Why?" Since the teacher I lived with often told me that she would not want to live in Cane Road, I had assumed that this might be a wide-spread attitude. It is not. The first two questions elicited such replies as "there's no difference . . . all the same . . . don't matter which part." I then asked people if they would mind living in Cane Road; wage laborers, small farmers, and big farmers and entrepreneurs told me that all areas were the same and that they only preferred to live "on the main" rather than "in the bush." Moreover, most could not explain why their northerly neighbors supported the JLP. They would just say, for example, "All Cane Road people are Labourites. I never hear them talk anything else."

Until the early 1950's, most residents of both Cane Road and Coco Hill supported the PNP. This was particularly true in the general elections, when a popular black physician who practiced in the community ran for office on the PNP ticket. A major reason for the split was that the Member of Parliament and the Parish Councillor—for many years the PNP won both seats—obtained many services and improvements for Coco Hill and not for Cane Road.* For example, Coco Hill received electricity in 1949, Cane Road in 1967. The main road to Kingston was paved in the early 1950's, but the road to the north coast

---

* I am not certain why this was so, although the crossroads was considered to be the "capital" of the district and those who were in charge of development schemes might have felt it was natural to place various services there. Another possibility is that the more vocal PNP leaders lived in Coco Hill, not in Cane Road, and agitated for the improvements to be made in their own neighborhood.

was not paved until 1962. The post office was built in Coco Hill in 1956; Cane Road received a postal agency in 1963. A public catchment tank was built in Coco Hill in 1956; Cane Road finally got one in 1966. In addition, the primary school, the library, the health clinic, and the police station were built near the crossroads in Coco Hill. These benefits naturally cemented Coco Hill's loyalty to the PNP. Residents of Cane Road had to come to Coco Hill to use the government services, which meant a walk of two or three miles for many of them. The JLP capitalized on the apparent discrimination against Cane Road, promising to bring electricity, paved roads, and other benefits to Cane Road and stressing to its residents that they had been victimized by the PNP.

Despite these general political differences between the two parts of the community, individuals in Cane Road and Coco Hill are linked by various social ties. Residents of Cane Road must still come to Coco Hill to use many government services, and many in each area own land in the other section. Individuals in the two areas are related by ties of kinship, marriage, and association and church membership. There is also considerable intersectional mobility. In part because of these cross-cutting ties, people from the two sections generally tread lightly in political discussions, particularly at election time. Many told me that when they meet people from Cane Road during election time, they avoid political discussions and Cane Road residents expressed the same sentiment with regard to those in Coco Hill. As within the sections themselves, overt political conflict rarely develops between Cane Road Labourites and Coco Hill PNPs; when disputes erupt between individuals in opposite parties, they usually revolve around slights to prestige rather than politics itself. And in such cases where wage laborers and unsuccessful small farmers do feel victimized by the political parties, they are likely to feel hostile towards the "bigger shot," no matter what their party affiliation.

CONCLUSION

The primary significance of both the JLP and PNP to the villagers is that they provide their supporters with certain kinds of economic assistance. However, the benefits do not help the villagers or their children to achieve their goals of success, and therefore generate little enthusiasm. The villagers perceive that they are "sufferers" in Jamaican society and they feel victimized, not because they are members of the JLP or the PNP, but because they are poor farmers.

In only one case, that is, the division between Cane Road and Coco Hill, has politics become the symbol through which a local cleavage is perceived. In this case party affiliation coincides to some extent with status divisions in the community and is perceived in these terms by the villagers. Moreover, Cane Road was victimized for many years when the PNP was in power and has only begun to receive various kinds of government services from the Labour Party. However, politics rarely becomes the basis for interpersonal disputes among the community's residents, even among residents of Cane Road and Coco Hill. Rather, disputes occur between persons of similar status and they arise over slights to one's prestige. Primarily because of the nature of benefits—but also because both parties have patronage to distribute and because respected persons in the community may affiliate with either party—party affiliation is not a basis for prestige. Politics, therefore, rarely leads to or becomes an issue in local interpersonal disputes.

Conclusion

Jamaica is a modernizing and changing society. In the past two decades the expansion of the system of formal education, the growth of nonagricultural sectors of the economy, and the emergence of modern political parties have increased the number of desirable occupational roles and have provided new opportunities for members of the lower class to occupy these positions. New political elites stress that although Jamaica has many problems to solve on the way to modernization, the society is a dynamic and progressive one. Their goal is to provide everyone with an equal chance to get ahead and to share in the good things that life has to offer.

Even though these structural and ideological changes have had some impact on rural communities, my research in one such community, Coco Hill, reveals that the villagers' opportunities for occupational mobility have not greatly expanded. Although there have been important changes in political institutions, the advent of new political parties has not created new, valued openings for the villagers. Leaders of the political party branches derive little influence or prestige from this role outside the community. Although the benefits which the parties distribute to their supporters help some to eke out a daily living, they do not provide villagers with opportunities to alter their occupational status in the society.

As for education, the villagers are enthusiastic about new educational opportunities the government provides. They feel that education now "counts" since their children can realistically aspire to enter secondary school or to pass island-wide examinations and can therefore hope to advance in the occupational system. In fact, the major expression of the villagers' mobility aspirations is in their hopes for their children's educational and occupational success, and this future orientation is an important factor in minimizing real conflict over limited access to channels of mobility. Those who fail to realize their own mobility goals are able to transfer their own hopes to their children.

However, as I have also noted, not all children from the village go to secondary school or pass the JSC exams. Those villagers whose children are not successful in school often express their frustrations and disappointments through envy of those whose children are successful, envy which may lead to overt conflict. I have suggested that the expression of this envy in the form of disputes and quarrels with other villagers functions to reduce cleavages in the total society. Individuals vent their frustrated mobility aspirations onto other persons in the local social system, rather than question the values of the national society which determines status criteria, or the legitimacy of the institutions which provide only limited channels for mobility. Nor do they participate in open conflict against established authorities. Moreover, villagers perceive alternate means for their children's mobility, primarily through emigration to the United States or Canada or working out in low-status jobs in Kingston to accumulate funds to finance educational training later in life.

Despite the general increase in educational opportunities, only a small percentage of children in Coco Hill continue their education past primary school. For every child who goes to secondary school or passes the JSC exams, approximately seven remain behind in Coco Hill as unsuccessful scholars or make alternative plans to get ahead. Some manage to emigrate to the United States or Canada and others go to Kingston. However, the latter usually merely swell the ranks of the urban unemployed and often return to Coco Hill later in life, drawn by the lure of land, family, and friends.

The limitations on opportunities for occupational mobility are inherent in the ideologies and structure of the educational system. The educational institutions of the society are not designed to provide all with a secondary school education but merely to give every Jamaican an equal chance to compete for the limited number of places available in these schools. Moreover, even in Coco Hill success in school is closely correlated with income, land ownership, and occupation; children of white-collar workers and big farmers and entrepreneurs are more likely to qualify for secondary school than those of small farmers and wage laborers.

Thus, the majority probably will not be able to alter their occupational status through the educational system; those who remain behind in Coco Hill will follow a life style similar to that of their parents. Again, this is not to deny that such improvements as electricity and better roads have raised living standards in Coco Hill and other rural communities. But in comparison with the improvements in life style and facilities available to members of other classes in the society, rural villagers still are, and still perceive themselves to be, a deprived group.

DEVELOPMENT AND MODERNIZATION IN NEW STATES

Although these findings are of intrinsic interest, they may have still further implications if they can be generalized beyond the particular area studied. Indeed, the increase in mobility opportunities brought about by the expansion of educational facilities and the rise to power of new political elites are social changes that are not unique to Jamaica. Such changes accompany the process of modernization in many parts of the world. Thus several aspects of the Jamaican situation seem to be generally applicable. On the one hand, there is the subjective perception by the rural population of the importance of education as an avenue for getting ahead. On the other hand, if my analysis is correct, there is the likelihood that the mobility aspirations of a large portion of the population are bound to be frustrated. The manner in which these frustrations are expressed can vary; even in rural Jamaica the villagers may turn toward more open conflict with the established regime. What is crucial is that modernizing states are unlikely to be able to meet the high expectations of the population. In this regard, let us review some of the basic aspects of the complex process known as modernization.

By "modernization," sometimes called social and political development, I refer to "all those social and political changes that accompanied industrialization in many countries of Western civilization. Among these are urbanization, changes in occupational structure, social mobility, development of education—as well as political changes from absolutist institutions to responsible and representative governments, and from a laissez-faire to modern welfare state." [1]

Social mobility, then, is one characteristic associated with modernization, and reflects the impact of modernization on a society's stratification system. It is defined as the "process by which individuals move from one position to another in society—positions which by general

consent have been given specific hierarchical values." [2] The study of
this process involves not only the extent to which individuals move up
and down within the class/status hierarchy but also the primary and
secondary cultural and structural aspects of the societal stratification
system in which this mobility takes place. Following Lloyd Fallers'
terminology, the cultural aspects of stratification include the criteria on
which ranking is based, and thus those characteristics the individual
must acquire to move up in the scale, and ideas as to how allocation of
persons to highly valued roles should and does take place. The structural aspects of stratification include the actual differentiation of roles
in the society as well as the number and types of roles at the various
levels that are available for allocation. [3]

New states in the process of modernization undergo several
changes which have an impact on stratification and social mobility
within the stratification system. First, in terms of the occupational
system, independence has been followed by an expansion of modern
occupational structures. Although families continue to be important
agents of socialization and influence allocation to occupational roles,
there is, to an increasing extent, a separation of occupational roles
from domestic life, and their location in specialized structures such as
business firms and government bureaucracies. [4] In addition, specific
occupational structures and roles are becoming dominant features of
these societies and foci of stratification: "the fate of the domestic unit
itself, including its placement in the stratification system, depends
upon the performance of one or more of its members within and according to the norms of, an external occupational system that cuts
across kinship." [5]

However limited economic development may be, there is some
growth of industry, commerce, and government services. In the new
states, independence has meant that the highest political and administrative positions, once filled by colonial officials, are now available
to members of the society. This proliferation of new occupational roles
creates new, and highly valued, openings in the social system. At the
same time, high-ranking positions in the occupational systems of the
new states tend to be of the bureaucratic, rather than entrepreneurial,
type. There are several reasons for this: (1) in the new states, early
stages of economic modernization were initiated by European entrepreneurs rather than by indigenous businessmen; (2) modern commerce and industry have come to them in relatively large-scale forms
in which the salaried executive is the dominant figure; (3) the initiative for pushing further development is taken largely by the state
since the new states lack a strong indigenous private sector and are
"industrial latecomers." This has resulted in expanded bureaucracies
for administration and planning. [6]

The prominence of bureaucrats in the elites of the new states has meant that advanced educational training becomes an important qualification for high-level occupational roles. It is true that secondary schools had for some time trained personnel to fill modern occupational roles in many colonial countries, for as relatively advanced forms of industry, commerce, and civil service were transferred from the colonial powers, a need developed for individuals with specialized training. Further, in the colonial setting schools taught the language and customs of the Europeans who dominated the occupational structures. For those who wished to succeed occupationally, knowledge of the European culture was necessary for communication with their supervisors and managers. As these societies have intensified modernization processes, education has become even more important. As in Jamaica, there are undoubtedly ideological and political pressures for educational expansion in the new states. In many of the new states schools are especially important in transmitting new civic values to the population, values which include the criteria of evaluation of various societal positions. In addition, there is some need to train individuals for expanding and increasingly technical, professional, and skilled occupations. Moreover, as modernization proceeds, educational and other organizations themselves become increasingly specialized and require additional manpower.

Second, there are changes in the criteria on which ranking in the new states is based. To be sure, in many new states "traditional" norms are still strong and these norms are often reinforced in the struggles among aspiring leaders for political positions vacated by colonial administrators; "combatants" may stress certain ethnic, tribal, or religious attributes of their potential followers in an effort to mobilize backing. However, the spread of educational opportunities, conscious attempts by political elites to draw traditional groups into new political structures and to create a national culture, and the increase in the number of modern occupational roles available has meant that nationwide ranking systems tend to develop, with occupation as the primary basis of ranking. Although many of the qualities which symbolize high status may be patterned on characteristics associated with traditional elites, it is becoming more common for universal, Western middle-class criteria—what Raymond Smith has called "universal bureaucratic" [7]—to predominate. This is because modernization takes place in the context of an international system of stratification in which Western nations, occupying the highest ranking position, serve as the model.

Third, political changes affect ideas about how allocation of persons to prestigious occupational roles should and does take place. Political elites in the new states proclaim egalitarian principles which stress that all can aspire to high-ranking occupations and that it is the state's duty to provide individuals with the means to achieve their goals.[8] Since education is the major basis of allocation to these occupational roles, political leaders tend to promote equal—or at least less unequal—access to education.

In sum, a major change in the stratification of a society which may be labeled "modern" is that social mobility becomes an institutionalized part of the social order. While "pre-modern" or "traditional" societies did not lack social mobility, it was generally of a more limited type. It involved individual mobility into a relatively fixed number of high-ranking roles and often took place within local structures. The main impact of modernization, as I have shown, is that occupational differentiation and concomitant educational changes and political development provide new foci of stratification. In new and modernizing societies education has become a highly prized goal for the majority of the population because education is a qualification for well-paid and prestigious occupations. As Philip Foster notes in his study of education in Ghana, secondary education "commands entry to nearly all significant roles within the public service or even into the larger commercial companies as well as access into higher institutions such as the University. . . ."[9]

JAMAICA'S DISTINCTIVE HISTORY *

While the broad political and economic changes outlined above seem to occur in all developing countries, Jamaica appears unique in many ways. It does not face many of the problems confronting other new and modernizing societies. For example, there are several key political problems emphasized by many academic analysts: the problems of "legitimacy" which confront new rulers; and the complex factors involved in reintegrating "old societies" into a new and modern state. One such analyst, Edward Shils, writes:

> A modern society is not just a complex of modern institutions. It is a mode of integration of the whole society. It is a mode of relationship between the center and the periphery of the society. . . . It involves a greater participation by the masses in the values of the society, a more active role in the making of society-wide decisions, and a greater prominence in the consideration of the elite.[10]

* S. N. Eisenstadt has noted that "the different starting points of the processes of modernization . . . have greatly influenced the specific contours of . . . development and the problems encountered in the course of it." S. N. Eisenstadt, *Modernization: Protest and Change* (Englewood Cliffs, N.J.: Prentice-Hall, 1966), p. 2.

To Shils, a major difficulty which leaders in the new states face is that of establishing an effective government, "of organizing and maintaining a modern political apparatus, that is, a rationally conducted administration, a cadre of leaders grouped in the public form of a party system (whether in a one-party system or in a multiparty system), and a machinery of public order." [11] There is also a need to legitimate themselves before the people, to adapt traditional literary, moral, and artistic culture to the techniques and content of modern education, and to establish a national language.

Jamaican political leaders, however, do not face these problems. Unlike many of the new states, Jamaica has no indigenous population. The original inhabitants of the island, the Arawak Indians, were decimated by disease and overwork during the period of Spanish rule; when England captured the island in 1655, the Arawaks had been completely wiped out. Jamaica was a plantation colony, manned almost entirely by people introduced from Africa and Europe. The population is now overwhelmingly black with only small groups of East Indians, Chinese, Europeans, Jews, Syrians, and people of mixed origin. There are no traditional tribal, religious, or ethnic groups with firmly entrenched political elites who might challenge the existing political order. Nor is the population divided along linguistic lines. Members of the lower class speak a patois but understand standard English as used by members of the elite. There is therefore no need to establish a new national language, a serious problem in many African and Asian countries.

Furthermore, since the end of the nineteenth century the population has been incorporated into one civil society. The English deliberately sought to integrate the freed slaves into colonial society to provide a basis for social order. The superiority of English cultural traditions was stressed in the schools, churches, and courts throughout the island as part of an attempt to establish a common ideology which legitimized English rule. To a large extent, the population came to believe in the moral and cultural superiority of things English—life style, cultural characteristics, education, and skin color—and desired to emulate them.

Jamaica has many other institutional prerequisites for successful integration and rapid social change: a structurally weak kinship system; a free market in land and other capital resources; a well-developed legal system based on formally "rational" criteria. In addition, occupation has been a primary social identity in the society for more than a century and secondary education the major avenue for occupational advancement. Jamaica has had a structurally modern educational system since the end of the nineteenth century. Success in the educational system was formally based on merit and ability and the system was specialized and divided into three levels—primary, secondary, and university (at that time available abroad). The educational institutions transmitted civic values to the population, including criteria for evaluation of different societal positions. Finally, since 1866, when the Colonial Office assumed power, the idea was institutionalized that it was the duty of the central government to provide certain services to the population.

Further, Jamaica does not appear to face major difficulty in rooting out certain traditional values which impede successful modernization—another problem stressed by some academic commentators in discussing new states. These analysts postulate that once the population adopts modern values and attitudes, it will be able to learn the skills necessary in the new institutional arrangements. In fact, one proponent of this view, David Apter, defines a modern state as one in which individuals have adopted modern values:

> At a minimum, modernization means that two conditions are present . . . : a social system that can constantly innovate without falling apart, including in innovation beliefs about the acceptability of change and, as well, social structures so differentiated as not to be inflexible; and second, a social framework that can provide the skills and knowledge necessary for living in a technologically advanced world, including the ability to communicate in terms of the technology.[12]

My research in Coco Hill reveals that rural Jamaicans are modern in the sense that they are oriented to "upliftment," change, and progress and are anxious to acquire the skills needed for occupational advancement. They seek to enter the modern sector of the economy and to escape from semi-subsistence agriculture—a desire they have had for many years. Many have sought advancement by emigrating, working abroad, or migrating to Kingston, and all are anxious that their children benefit from the new educational opportunities.*

Yet despite these many modern features and despite the absence of certain difficulties that impede modernization in other new states, Jamaica still faces major problems which at the national level prevent

---

* This is not to deny that some rural villagers—particularly those of lowest status in their communities—continue to adhere to certain traditional beliefs and practices which may impede mobility. The investigation of why these villagers do not conform to certain dominant cultural traditions or adopt attitudes and behavior that would appear to facilitate occupational advancement is a complex and fascinating area for study. It is beyond the scope of this book to examine the influence of all the varied and interrelated forces which are involved. One important factor, however, is their low economic status and accompanying belief that the chances for altering their own or their children's status are remote.

full development and at the local level result in blockages to upward mobility. I suggest that the key problems facing Jamaica stem primarily from the structure of the island's economy and the island's relation to other nations in an international economic, political, and social system. These problems, which are shared by many new and moderniz ing states, are more sharply revealed in Jamaica because it is not torn by communal strife, does not face the problem of legitimacy, and has a population which has been oriented to a modern occupational system for many years.

A major difficulty is that Jamaica, like many developing nations, has achieved only a minimal degree of industrialization and therefore cannot meet the demands for higher-level occupational roles. As Reinhard Bendix points out, modernization and industrialization may be considered analytically as two distinct processes and may proceed at different rates within a country. Development refers both to economic changes "brought about by a technology based on inanimate sources of power as well as on the continuous development of applied scientific research," [13] and to those social and political changes listed above as characteristics of modernization. Thus, societies which have modern features such as fairly well developed educational systems but which have attained only a minimal degree of industrialization, cannot be considered developed.

Nations can remain underdeveloped for several reasons, among them a lack of resources—primarily capital—and their continued economic dependence on more developed nations. Irving Louis Horowitz notes that economic development in nations of what he terms the Third World is limited because of their position in a world stratification system and their economic and political relations with major world powers. For example, nations of the Third World supply world markets with such primary commodities as unprocessed agricultural products and nonferrous metals and are dependent on major powers, not only for direct fiscal support, but for prices paid for raw materials, costs of importing goods, and control of international trade and money markets.[14]

It is true that there has been some expansion of the nonagricultural sectors of the Jamaican economy in recent years with developments in mining, industry, light manufacturing, and tourism, as well as an increase in government services. However, as Gordon Lewis writes of the whole Caribbean region, the Jamaican economy exhibits "in exaggerated form, all the major properties of the colonial regime —foreign ownership and control in the major sectors of . . . sugar, banking, insurance, mining and manufacturing; external decision-making with respect to investment and allocation of resources by the head offices of the big multinational corporations; structural unemployment and underemployment, combined with high salary–wage levels in privileged sectors; separation between local extraction of raw materials and overseas manufacture of the finished product; lack of indigenous technology; and the concentration by overseas wealth in capital-oriented industries that do little to absorb the labor surplus inherited from the old plantation economy." [15]

Thus, the bulk of the profits of Jamaica's major industries—bauxite and light manufacturing—leave the country. Moreover, these industries, which contribute the most to the national income, which are constantly cited by government officials as indices of progress, and which give Jamaicans the impression that there are many new well-paid jobs available, have opened up relatively few new jobs. For example, the bauxite industry was nonexistent in 1950. By 1967 the mining sector of the economy accounted for 10 per cent of the gross domestic product and 47 per cent of domestic exports. However, due to its capital-intensive nature and the fact that most of the bauxite is processed abroad, it employs less than one per cent of the labor force, and foreign ownership means that only 50 per cent of the value of its output accrues to Jamaica residents.[16] Similarly, by 1966, 149 factories had been established under the incentive laws designed to attract foreign capital. Although exports of manufactured goods increased from £850,000 in 1955 to more than £6.0 million in 1965, the total employment in industries established under these incentive laws was only about 9,000.[17]

In contrast to many other developing states, the Jamaican government has not taken a major role in economic development. Its economic development activities tend to be confined to providing incentives for private Jamaican and international companies, and some very limited monetary control. The advantages to foreign firms which the leaders emphasize to attract foreign capital include tax-free holidays, freedom from fiscal controls, and the availability of cheap labor. However, as mentioned above, because of the capital-intensive nature of these industries, relatively few new jobs are created.

Jamaican leaders point out that a major hope for the island's economy is increased agricultural production. They note that the island's hotels rely on foreign produce to feed hotel guests and that more than 25 per cent of the island's food needs are supplied by imports. They have tried to instill in the bulk of the population a commitment to agriculture, a desire to stay on the land and to take pride in agricultural work, but their attempts have largely failed. As I have shown, the villagers of Coco Hill, typical in this respect of rural villagers throughout the island, want to leave the land and to enter nonagricultural occupations. They realize that small-scale farming is considered a low-status occupation, that it cannot support desired life styles, and that rural areas do not offer the amenities available in the towns and cities.

Thus, in seeking to reorient the population to accept and enjoy agricultural work, the government attempts, in effect, to alter the mod ern values of the population and to create a peasant class, happy to work on the land and content to send a small number of its most able children to secondary school to join the ranks of the elite. However, this conflicts with the basic goals of the villagers. It is precisely because there are more opportunities for entering nonagricultural occupations that the villagers feel there has been some progress in the country, and they hope that these opportunities will be expanded in the future.

Even if Jamaica should attempt to expand its industrialized sector or if the government were to institute radical nationalization policies, it would still face many difficulties. In the first place, the island has neither the natural resources nor the capital for industrial development. And it is unlikely that political leaders will attempt nationalization since the government is restricted in policy decisions by close economic and political ties to the United States, Canada, and England.

Thus, there is a fundamental contradiction within the social structure of Jamaican society. On the one hand, implicit in the values supporting the stratification system is the image of the "admirable man" which is accepted by the population, that is, a man who can maintain a life style similar to that of the North American middle classes and who can consume imported American goods. On the other hand, the economic structure cannot realistically provide the means for the vast majority of the population to realize their aspirations. The problems arising from this contradiction may be especially acute in Jamaica for many reasons: its proximity to the United States; the presence of large numbers of American tourists; the emigration of many Jamaicans to the United States and Canada and their subsequent return; the island's small size and good communications network, which enhance the visibility of members of the elite and their consumption patterns. Ivan Illich, an observer of underdevelopment in Latin America, puts the problem well when he speaks of underdevelopment as a state of mind: "when mass needs are converted to the demand for new brands of packaged solutions which are forever beyond the reach of the majority . . . . The ruling groups in these countries build up services which have been designed for an affluent culture; once they have monopolized demand in this way, they can never satisfy majority needs." [18]

At present the villagers are optimistic about the new opportunities available to them and they feel that there are more ways to "get on" in the society. Although there will be some additional occupational openings available, it is not likely that they will increase in number as quickly as the demand for them grows. The probability is that most rural villagers will not alter their occupational status but will continue to follow occupations and life styles not too different from those of their parents. This helps to explain the persistence of certain traditional beliefs and practices at the local level. Moreover, the fact that the younger generation has been given increased educational opportunities and that politicians continually emphasize the improvements in the society, may lead them to be more frustrated in their failures than the older generation. These frustrated aspirations of the lower class can seriously strain the political system. Thus far, disappointments and frustrations have been expressed in ways which for the most part have not threatened the stability of the system—through violence towards other members of the lower class, for example, magic, and religion. Moreover, emigration has drained off excess population and provided an alternative means of mobility for many.

At present, the situation is far from chaotic. The majority of the population does not question the legitimacy of the societal institutions and even the most radical groups do not advocate violence as a means to effect the changes they desire. As Raymond Smith writes, the stability of the "two-party democratic system" depends on the ability of the parties "to recognize the legitimacy of each other's actions and to confine their supporters' activities to the polls without permitting or encouraging physical violence, and—most important—upon the ability of the government in power to cope with outbreaks of violence from a growing population (which is being frustrated in its aspirations) while at the same time maintaining democratic institutions intact." [19] While there may not be major changes in the economy, there may be sufficient changes to forestall major conflicts.

IMPLICATIONS FOR OTHER NEW NATIONS

It appears likely that along with the problems of legitimacy, political integration, and reorienting the population to a set of modern values that confront most new nations, other developing states may face additional difficulties which Jamaica has encountered in its experience with modernization and change. For example, the fact that most new nations have not been fully able to modernize their economies means that they too can offer only a limited number of new occupational roles to societal members. In fact, tribal, religious, and racial conflicts often arise over competition for these new, scarce, and desired occupations and politicians may exploit the discontents of

unsuccessful groups in their effort to gain power. In addition, in most
new nations, improved world and national communications and attempts by political elites to draw traditional groups into the "new
states" have meant that the bulk of the population is becoming oriented
to Western consumption patterns, patterns which only a small elite
can afford to maintain.

Even if these nations were to solve many of the problems imped-
ing modernization, they would still face major difficulties. Should
they be successful in inculcating achievement values or should they
resolve tribal and other conflicts, it seems unlikely that they have the
ability to solve basic economic problems in the near future. Like
Jamaica, they do not appear to have the capital to spur economic
development on their own nor is it likely that they will get it from
other nations. Indeed, as Gunnar Myrdal has pointed out, the only
viable path to development for the underdeveloped nations of the
world is a "forceful rise in the share of the national income which is
withheld from consumption and devoted to investment."[20] This "becomes a much more difficult policy in the underdeveloped countries
today than it ever was in the now highly developed ones in their early
stages of economic development. This is so both because of their much
greater poverty and because of the new ideology—which had no real
counterpart in the earlier history of the developed countries but has
now been spread with their generous support—that the purpose of
economic development is to raise levels of living for the masses of
the people."[21]

If these analyses are correct, then it appears reasonable to gen-
eralize from the Jamaican situation. The problems of economic development may appear in pristine purity in Jamaica, but the impediments
to such development seem to confront many new nations. This is not
to say that economic development eliminates social and economic
inequalities. The most advanced industrial nations still have class and
status differences, but these countries do have a general standard of
living and degree of mobility which many leaders and the general
population in the less developed countries would like to emulate. What
is problematic is their ability to follow the path of the developed nations. This present study indicates some of the ramifications of such
problems in one small Jamaican community. To the extent that Jamaica
does share with other new and developing countries the basic difficulties that I have discussed, it seems profitable for anthropologists
studying change in local communities in other new states to give serious weight both to structural blockages which impede mobility and
change and to the impact of these blockages on the social and political
life of the residents.

Notes

NOTES TO INTRODUCTION

[1] Joseph Schumpeter, *Imperialism and Social Classes*, Meridian Books (New York and Cleveland: World Publishing Company, 1955), p. 111.

[2] Gordon Lewis, quoted in Raymond T. Smith in "Social Stratification in the Caribbean," in *Essays in Comparative Social Stratification*, ed. Leonard Plotnicov and Arthur Tuden (Pittsburgh: University of Pittsburgh Press, 1970), p. 51.

[3] Clifford Geertz, *Peddlars and Princes* (Chicago: University of Chicago Press, 1963), p. 4.

[4] Geertz, "Religion and Social Change: A Javanese Example," in *Reader in Comparative Religion*, ed. William A. Lessa and Evon Z. Vogt (2nd ed.; New York: Harper and Row, 1965), p. 549.

[5] See Judith Blake, *Family Structure in Jamaica* (New York: The Free Press of Glencoe, 1961), Edith Clarke, *My Mother Who Fathered Me* (2nd ed.; London: George Allen and Unwin, 1966), Yehudi Cohen, "Four Categories of Interpersonal Relationships in the Family and Community in a Jamaican Village," *Anthropological Quarterly*, III (October, 1955), 121–147, G. E. Cumper, "The Jamaican Family: Village and Estate," *Social and Economic Studies*, VII (March, 1958), 76–108, William Davenport, "The Family System of Jamaica," *Social and Economic Studies*, X (December, 1961), 420–454, Fernando Henriques, *Family and Colour in Jamaica* (London: MacGibbon and Kee, 1953), Madeline Kerr, *Personality and Conflict in Jamaica* (2nd ed.; London: Collins, 1963).

[6] See F. G. Cassidy, *Jamaica Talk: Three Hundred Years of the English Language in Jamaica* (London: Macmillan, 1961), F. G. Cassidy and R. B. LePage, *Dictionary of Jamaican English* (Cambridge: Cambridge University Press, 1967), R. B. LePage and David DeCamp, *Jamaican Creole: An Historical Introduction to Jamaican Creole, and Four Jamaican Creole Texts* (London: Macmillan, 1960).

[7] See Louise Bennett, *Anancy Stories and Dialect Verse* (Kingston: Pioneer Press, 1957), Walter Jekyll, *Jamaican Song and Story* (London: David Nutt, Publication of the Folklore Society, 1907), Philip M. Sherlock, *Anansi the Spider Man: Jamaican Folk Tales* (London: Macmillan, 1956).

[8] See Martha Warren Beckwith, *Black Roadways: A Study of Jamaican Folk Life* (New York: New American Library, 1970), G. E. Simpson, "Jamaican Revivalist Cults," *Social and Economic Studies*, V (December, 1956), 321–442.

[9] See Clarke, *op. cit.*, Lambros Comitas, "Occupational Multiplicity in Rural Jamaica," *Proceedings of the American Ethnological Society*, ed. Viola Garfield and Ernestine Friedl (Seattle: University of Washington Press, 1964), pp. 41–50, G. E. Cumper, "A Modern Jamaican Sugar Estate," *Social and Economic Studies*, III (June, 1954), 119–160, David Edwards, *An Economic Study of Small Farming in Jamaica* (Kingston: Institute of Social and Economic Research, University College of the West Indies, 1961), Margaret Katzin, "The Jamaican Country Higgler," *Social and Economic Studies*, VIII (December, 1959), 421–440 and "The Business of Higglering in Jamaica," *Social and Economic Studies*, IX (September, 1960), 297–331, Sidney Mintz, "The Jamaican Internal Marketing Pattern," *Social and Economic Studies*, IV (March, 1955), 95–103, Sidney Mintz and Douglas Hall, "The Origins of the Jamaican Internal Marketing System," Yale University Publications in Anthropology, No. 57 (New Haven: Department of Anthropology, Yale University, 1960).

[10] There has been little written about politics or education in Jamaican rural communities. Madeline Kerr devotes a chapter to politics and a chapter to the school in her study of three Jamaican rural communities carried out in the late 1940's, *op. cit.* M. G. Smith discusses formal and informal leadership patterns in "Community Organization in Rural Jamaica," in M. G. Smith, *The Plural Society in the British West Indies* (Los Angeles: University of California Press, 1965), pp. 176–195. For description and analyses of education in rural Jamaica see O. N. Bolland, "Literacy in a Rural Area of Jamaica," *Social and Economic Studies*, XX (March, 1071), 28–51; Edward Seaga, "Parent-Teacher Relationships in a Jamaican Village," *Social and Economic Studies*, III (December, 1955), 289–302; M. G. Smith, "Education and Occupational Choice in Rural Jamaica," in M. G. Smith, *op. cit.*, pp. 196–220. See also Nancy Foner, "Competition, Conflict, and Education in Rural Jamaica," *Human Organization*, XXXI (Winter, 1972) and "Party Politics in a Jamaican Community," *Caribbean Studies*, forthcoming.

NOTES TO CHAPTER I

[1] George W. Roberts, "Demographic Aspects of Rural Development: The Jamaican Experience," *Social and Economic Studies*, XVII (September, 1968), 278.

[2] Talcott Parsons, in the Introduction to *The Theory of Social and Economic Organization*, by Max Weber (New York: The Free Press, 1964), p. 13.

[3] See Davenport, *op. cit.*, pp. 447–454 and Clarke, *op. cit.*, pp. 33–71 for a fuller description of land tenure in rural Jamaica.

⁴ For a discussion of internal migration see G. E. Cumper, "Population Movements in Jamaica—1830–1950," *Social and Economic Studies,* IV (September, 1956), 261–280.

⁵ Gloria Cumper, "In Search of a New Identity," *The Times* (London: September 26, 1968), p. 1.

NOTE TO CHAPTER II

¹ Thorstein Veblen, "The Theory of the Leisure Class," in *Class, Status, and Power,* ed. R. Bendix and S. M. Lipset (2nd ed.; New York: The Free Press, 1966), p. 37.

NOTES TO CHAPTER III

¹ Raymond T. Smith, "Social Stratification, Cultural Pluralism and Integration in West Indian Societies," *Caribbean Integration—Papers on Social, Political and Economic Integration,* ed. Sybil Lewis and Thomas G. Mathews (Rio Piedras: Institute of Caribbean Studies, University of Puerto Rico, 1967), p. 232. For a fuller treatment of this process see *ibid.,* pp. 229–233.

² "Report of Sterling to the British Government, 11 May 1835," in Shirley Gordon, *A Century of West Indian Education—A Source Book* (London: Longmans, 1963), pp. 20–21.

³ R. T. Smith, "Social Stratification, Cultural Pluralism and Integration in West Indian Societies," p. 235.

⁴ Lloyd Fallers, "Equality, Modernity, and Democracy in the New States," in *Old Societies and New States,* ed. Clifford Geertz (New York: Free Press of Glencoe, 1963), p. 162.

⁵ R. T. Smith, "Social Stratification in the Caribbean," pp. 45–46.

⁶ Elsa V. Goveia, *Slave Society in the British Leeward Islands at the End of the Eighteenth Century* (New Haven: Yale University Press, 1965), p. 225.

⁷ *Ibid.,* p. 226.

⁸ R. T. Smith, "Social Stratification in the Caribbean," p. 53.

⁹ Eisner, *op. cit.,* p. 331.

¹⁰ R. T. Smith, "Social Stratification in the Caribbean," p. 48.

¹¹ See Hall, *op. cit.,* and Eisner, *op. cit.,* for a fuller discussion of economic conditions in post-emancipation Jamaica.

¹² Cf. Foster, *op. cit.,* pp. 183–185.

¹³ *The Daily Gleaner* (Kingston), June 5, 1969.

¹⁴ *Ibid.,* November 12, 1969.

¹⁵ O. C. Francis, *The People of Modern Jamaica* (Kingston: Department of Statistics, 1963).

NOTES TO CHAPTER IV

[1] Joyce Gladwell, *Brown Face, Big Master* (London: Inter-Varsity Press, 1969), p. 33.

[2] Seymour Martin Lipset and Reinhard Bendix, *Social Mobility in Industrial Society* (Berkeley and Los Angeles: University of California Press, 1959), pp. 262–263.

[3] *Ibid.*, p. 263.

[4] M. G. Smith, "Education and Occupational Choice in Rural Jamaica," in M. C. Smith, *op. cit.*, p. 219.

NOTES TO CHAPTER V

[1] R. T. Smith, "A Preliminary Report on a Study of Selected Groups of East Indians in Jamaica," unpublished paper, p. 14.

[2] Davenport, *op. cit.*, p. 440.

NOTES TO CHAPTER VI

[1] Robert Merton, "Patterns of Influence: Local and Cosmopolitan Influentials," in *Social Theory and Social Structure* (New York: The Free Press of Glencoe, 1957), p. 400.

[2] *Ibid.*

[3] Cf. M. G. Smith, "Community Organization in Rural Jamaica," in M. G. Smith, *op. cit.*, p. 188.

NOTES TO CHAPTER VII

[1] R. T. Smith, "Social Stratification, Cultural Pluralism and Integration in West Indian Societies," p. 242.

[2] See C. Paul Bradley, "Mass Parties in Jamaica," *Social and Economic Studies*, IX (December, 1960), 375–417. Two recent publications which deal with political changes in this period have appeared since this manuscript was completed: Trevor Munroe, *The Politics of Constitutional Decolonization: Jamaica, 1944–1962* (Kingston: Institute of Social and Economic Research, University of the West Indies, 1972), and Rex Nettleford, *Manley and the Politics of Jamaica—Towards an analysis of political change in Jamaica, 1938–1968*, Supplement to *Social and Economic Studies*, XX (September, 1971).

[3] Clifford Geertz, "The Integrative Revolution," in *Old Societies and New States*, p. 120.

[4] Gordon K. Lewis, *The Growth of the Modern West Indies* (London: MacGibbon and Kee, 1968), p. 184.

[5] *Ibid.*

NOTES TO CONCLUSION

[1] Reinhard Bendix, *Nation-Building and Citizenship: Studies of Our Changing Social Order*, Anchor Books (Garden City, N.Y.: Doubleday, 1969), p. 6. Bendix does not assume that modernization constitutes a universal evolutionary process resulting from internal societal development alone. It can also occur as a result of international emulation. Other writers have often treated modernizing states as if they can be analyzed without more than a passing reference to linkages to other nations in a wider, international system. See Reinhard Bendix, "Tradition and Modernity Reconsidered," *Comparative Studies in Society and History*, IX (April, 1967), 292–346.

[2] Lipset and Bendix, *op. cit.*, pp. 1–2.

[3] Fallers, *op. cit.*, pp. 162–168.

[4] *Ibid.*, p. 181.

[5] *Ibid.*, p. 182.

[6] *Ibid.*, pp. 185–187.

[7] R. T. Smith, "Social Stratification in the Caribbean," p. 63.

[8] Fallers, *op. cit.*, pp. 205–206.

[9] Foster, *op. cit.*, p. 197.

[10] Edward Shils, "On the Comparative Study of New States," in *Old Societies and New States*, p. 21.

[11] *Ibid.*, p. 2.

[12] David Apter, "Political Religion in the New Nations," in *Old Societies and New States*, p. 62.

[13] Bendix, *Nation-Building and Citizenship*, p. 6.

[14] Irving Louis Horowitz, *Three Worlds of Development—The Theory and Practice of International Stratification* (New York: Oxford University Press, 1966), p. 26. See also Gunnar Myrdal, *Economic Theory and Underdeveloped Regions*, Harper Torchbooks (New York: Harper and Row, 1971).

[15] Gordon K. Lewis, "The Politics of the Caribbean," in *The United States and the Caribbean*, ed. Tad Szulc, Spectrum Books (Englewood Cliffs, N.J.: Prentice Hall, 1971), p. 34. See also Frank McDonald, "The Commonwealth Caribbean," *ibid.*, pp. 126–156.

[16] Owen Jefferson, "Some Aspects of the Post-War Economic Development of Jamaica," *New World Quarterly*, III (High Season, 1967), 4. Since this manuscript was completed a book by Owen Jefferson on the above subject has been published: *Post-War Economic Development of Jamaica* (Kingston: Institute of Social and Economic Research, University of the West Indies, 1972). Also recently published in this series are George

Beckford, *Persistent Poverty* (Kingston: Institute of Social and Economic Research, University of the West Indies, 1972) and Norman Girvan, *Foreign Capital and Economic Underdevelopment in Jamaica* (Kingston: Institute of Social and Economic Research, University of the West Indies, 1972).

[17] Jefferson, "Some Aspects of the Post-War Economic Development of Jamaica," *ibid.*

[18] Ivan Illich, "Outwitting the 'Developed' Countries," *The New York Review of Books*, XIII (November 6, 1969), 22.

[19] R. T. Smith, "Social Stratification in the Caribbean," p. 68.

[20] Myrdal, *op. cit.*, p. 84.

[21] *Ibid.*, p. 85.

References

Apter, David. "Political Religion in the New Nations." *Old Societies and New States*. Edited by Clifford Geertz. New York: The Free Press of Glencoe, 1963. Pp. 57–104.

Beckford, George. *Persistent Poverty*. Kingston: Institute of Social and Economic Research, University of the West Indies, 1972.

Beckwith, Martha Warren. *Black Roadways: A Study of Jamaican Folk Life*. Afro-American Studies. New York: New American Library, 1970.

Bendix, Reinhard. "Tradition and Modernity Reconsidered." *Comparative Studies in Society and History*, IX (April, 1967), 292–346.

———. *Nation-Building and Citizenship: Studies of Our Changing Social Order*. Anchor Books. Garden City, N.Y.: Doubleday, 1969.

Bennett, Louise. *Anancy Stories and Dialect Verse*. Kingston: Pioneer Press, 1957.

Blake, Judith. *Family Structure in Jamaica*. New York: The Free Press of Glencoe, 1961.

Bolland, O. N. "Literacy in a Rural Area of Jamaica." *Social and Economic Studies*, XX (March, 1971), 28–51.

Bradley, C. Paul. "Mass Parties in Jamaica." *Social and Economic Studies*, IX (December, 1960), 375–417.

Braithwaite, Lloyd. "Social Stratification in Trinidad." *Social and Economic Studies*, II (October, 1953), 5–175.

———. "Social Stratification and Cultural Pluralism." *Social and Cultural Pluralism in the Caribbean*. Edited by Vera Rubin. New York: Annals of the New York Academy of Sciences, 1960. Pp. 816–831.

Bryce-Laporte, R. S. "M. G. Smith's Version of Pluralism—The Questions it Raises." *Comparative Studies in Society and History*, X (October, 1967), 114–120.

Cassidy, F. G. *Jamaica Talk: Three Hundred Years of the English Language in Jamaica*. London: Macmillan, 1961.

———, and LePage, R. B. *Dictionary of Jamaican English*. Cambridge: Cambridge University Press, 1967.

Clarke, Edith. *My Mother Who Fathered Me.* 2nd ed. London: George Allen and Unwin, 1966.

Cohen, Yehudi. "Four Categories of Interpersonal Relationships in the Family and Community in a Jamaican Village." *Anthropological Quarterly,* III (October, 1955), 121–147.

Comitas, Lambros. "Occupational Multiplicity in Rural Jamaica." *Proceedings of the American Ethnological Society, 1963.* Edited by Viola Garfield and Ernestine Friedl. Seattle: University of Washington Press, 1964. Pp. 41–50.

Cross, Malcolm. "Cultural Pluralism and Sociological Theory: A Critique and Re-evaluation." *Social and Economic Studies,* XVII (December, 1968), 381–397.

Cumper, G. E. "A Modern Jamaican Sugar Estate." *Social and Economic Studies,* III (September, 1954), 119–160.

———. "Population Movements in Jamaica, 1830–1950." *Social and Economic Studies,* V (September, 1956), 261–280.

———. "The Jamaican Family: Village and Estate." *Social and Economic Studies,* VII (March, 1958), 76–108.

Cumper, Gloria. "In Search of a New Identity." *The Times* (London). September 26, 1968.

Curtin, Philip. *Two Jamaicas: The Role of Ideas in a Tropical Colony, 1830–1865.* Cambridge, Mass.: Harvard University Press, 1955.

Davenport, William. "The Family System of Jamaica." *Social and Economic Studies,* X (December, 1961), 420–454.

Edwards, David. *An Economic Study of Small Farming in Jamaica.* Kingston: Institute of Social and Economic Research, University College of the West Indies, 1961.

Eisenstadt, S. N. *Modernization: Protest and Change.* Englewood Cliffs, N.J.: Prentice-Hall, 1966.

Eisner, Gisela. *Jamaica 1830–1930: A Study in Economic Growth.* Manchester: Manchester University Press, 1961.

Fallers, Lloyd A. "Equality, Modernity, and Democracy in the New States." *Old Societies and New States.* Edited by Clifford Geertz. New York: The Free Press of Glencoe, 1963. Pp. 158–219.

Foner, Nancy. "Competition, Conflict, and Education in Rural Jamaica." *Human Organization,* XXXI (Winter, 1972).

———. "Party Politics in a Jamaican Community." *Caribbean Studies.* Forthcoming.

Foster, Philip. *Education and Social Change in Ghana.* Chicago: University of Chicago Press, 1965.

Francis, O. C. *The People of Modern Jamaica.* Kingston: Department of Statistics, 1963.

Geertz, Clifford. "The Integrative Revolution." *Old Societies and New States.* Edited by Clifford Geertz. New York: The Free Press of Glencoe, 1963. Pp. 105–157.

————. *Peddlars and Princes.* Chicago: University of Chicago Press, 1963.

————. "Religion and Social Change: A Javanese Example." *Reader in Comparative Religion.* Edited by William A. Lessa and Evon Z. Vogt. 2nd ed. New York: Harper and Row, 1965. Pp. 547–559.

Gerth, H. and Mills, C. Wright. *From Max Weber: Essays in Sociology.* Galaxy Books. New York: Oxford University Press, 1958.

Girvan, Norman. *Foreign Capital and Economic Underdevelopment in Jamaica.* Kingston: Institute of Social and Economic Research, University of the West Indies, 1972.

Gladwell, Joyce. *Brown Face, Big Master.* London: Inter-Varsity Press, 1969.

Gordon, Shirley C. *A Century of West Indian Education—A Source Book.* London: Longmans, 1963.

Goveia, Elsa V. *Slave Society in the British Leeward Islands at the End of the Eighteenth Century.* New Haven: Yale University Press, 1965.

Hall, Douglas. *Free Jamaica, 1838–1865—An Economic History.* New Haven: Yale University Press, 1959.

Hart, Richard. "Jamaica and Self-Determination, 1660–1970." *Race,* XIII (January, 1972), 271–297.

Henriques, Fernando. *Family and Colour in Jamaica.* London: MacGibbon and Kee, 1953.

Horowitz, Irving Louis. *Three Worlds of Development—The Theory and Practice of International Stratification.* New York: Oxford University Press, 1966.

Illich, Ivan. "Outwitting the 'Developed' Countries." *The New York Review of Books,* XIII (November 6, 1969), 20–24.

Jayawardena, Chandra. *Conflict and Solidarity in a Guianese Plantation.* London: The Athlone Press, University of London, 1963.

Jefferson, Owen. "Some Aspects of the Post-War Economic Development of Jamaica," *New World Quarterly,* III (High Season, 1967), 1–11.

————. *The Post-War Economic Development of Jamaica.* Kingston: Institute of Social and Economic Research, University of the West Indies, 1972.

Jekyll, Walter. *Jamaican Song and Story.* Publication of the Folklore Society, No. 55. London: David Nutt, 1907.

Katzin, Margaret. "The Jamaican Country Higgler." *Social and Economic Studies,* VIII (December, 1959), 421–435.

————. "The Business of Higglering in Jamaica." *Social and Economic Studies,* IX (September, 1960), 297–331.

Kelly, J. B. "The Jamaican Independence Constitution of 1962." *Caribbean Studies,* III (April, 1963), 18–83.

Kerr, Madeline. *Personality and Conflict in Jamaica*. 2nd ed. London: Collins, 1963.

LePage, R. B. and DeCamp, David. *Jamaican Creole: An Historical Introduction to Jamaican Creole, and Four Jamaican Creole Texts*. London: Macmillan, 1960.

Lewis, Gordon K. *The Growth of the Modern West Indies*. London: MacGibbon and Kee, 1968.

————. "The Politics of the Caribbean." *The United States and the Caribbean*. Edited by Tad Szulc. Spectrum Books. Englewood Cliffs, N.J.: Prentice-Hall, 1971. Pp. 5–35.

Lipset, Seymour Martin and Bendix, Reinhard. *Social Mobility in Industrial Society*. Berkeley and Los Angeles: University of California Press, 1959.

McDonald, Frank. "The Commonwealth Caribbean." *The United States and the Caribbean*. Edited by Tad Szulc. Spectrum Books. Englewood Cliffs, N.J.: Prentice-Hall, 1971. Pp. 126–156.

McKenzie, H. I. "The Plural Society Debate: Some Comments on a Recent Contribution." *Social and Economic Studies*, XV (March, 1966), 53–60.

Merton, Robert. "Patterns of Influence: Local and Cosmopolitan Influentials." *Social Theory and Social Structure*. Glencoe, Ill.: The Free Press, 1957. Pp. 387–420.

Mintz, Sidney. "The Jamaican Internal Marketing Pattern." *Social and Economic Studies*, IV (March, 1955), 95–103.

————, and Hall, Douglas. "The Origins of the Jamaican Internal Marketing System." *Yale University Publications in Anthropology*, No. 57. New Haven: Yale University Press, 1960.

Munroe, Trevor. *The Politics of Constitutional Decolonization: Jamaica, 1944–1962*. Kingston: Institute of Social and Economic Research, University of the West Indies, 1972.

Myrdal, Gunnar. *Economic Theory and Underdeveloped Regions*. Harper Torchbooks. New York: Harper and Row, 1971.

Nettleford, Rex. *Manley and the Politics of Jamaica—Towards an analysis of political change in Jamaica 1938–1968*. Supplement to *Social and Economic Studies*, XX (September, 1971), 1–72.

Paget, Hugh. "The Free Village System in Jamaica." *Caribbean Quarterly*, X (March, 1964), 38–51.

Phelps, O. W. "The Rise of the Labour Movement in Jamaica." *Social and Economic Studies*, IX (December, 1960), 417–467.

Post, K. W. J. "The Politics of Protest in Jamaica, 1938." *Social and Economic Studies*, XVIII (December, 1969), 374–390.

Roberts, G. W. "Demographic Aspects of Rural Development: The Jamaican Experience." *Social and Economic Studies*, XVII (September, 1968), 276–283.

Rubin, Vera. "Social and Cultural Pluralism by M. G. Smith." *Social and Cultural Pluralism in the Caribbean.* Edited by Vera Rubin. New York: Annals of the New York Academy of Sciences, 1960. Pp. 780–785.

Schumpeter, Joseph. *Imperialism and Social Classes.* Meridian Books. New York and Cleveland: World Publishing Co., 1955.

Seaga, Edward. "Parent-Teacher Relationships in a Jamaican Village." *Social and Economic Studies,* III (December, 1955), 289–302.

Sherlock, Philip M. *Anansi the Spider Man: Jamaican Folk Tales.* London: Macmillan, 1956.

Shils, Edward. "On the Comparative Study of the New States." *Old Societies and New States.* Edited by Clifford Geertz. New York: The Free Press of Glencoe, 1963. Pp. 1–26.

———. "Deference." *Social Stratification.* Edited by J. A. Jackson. Cambridge: Cambridge University Press, 1968. Pp. 104–132.

Simpson, G. E. "Jamaican Revivalist Cults." *Social and Economic Studies,* V (December, 1956), 321–442.

Smith, M. G. *The Plural Society in the British West Indies.* Los Angeles: University of California Press, 1965.

Smith, Raymond T. "A Preliminary Report on a Study of Selected Groups of East Indians in Jamaica." Unpublished paper, n.d.

———. Review of *Social and Cultural Pluralism in the Caribbean. American Anthropologist,* LXIII (February, 1961), 155–157.

———. "People and Change." *New World: Guyana Independence Issue.* (Demerara, Guyana, May, 1966), 49–54.

———. "Social Stratification, Cultural Pluralism, and Integration in West Indian Societies." *Caribbean Integration—Papers on Social, Political, and Economic Integration.* Edited by Sybil Lewis and Thomas G. Mathews. Rio Piedras: Institute of Caribbean Studies, University of Puerto Rico, 1967. Pp. 226–258.

———. "Social Stratification in the Caribbean." *Essays in Comparative Social Stratification.* Edited by Leonard Plotnicov and Arthur Tuden. Pittsburgh: University of Pittsburgh Press, 1970. Pp. 43–77.

Veblen, Thorstein. "The Theory of the Leisure Class." *Class, Status, and Power.* Edited by Reinhard Bendix and Seymour Martin Lipset. 2nd ed. New York: The Free Press, 1966. Pp. 36–42.

Weber, Max. *The Theory of Social and Economic Organization.* New York: The Free Press of Glencoe, 1964.

Appendix

TABLE I

OCCUPATIONS OF ADULT MALES ON PERCY ROAD

A. *Occupations:*

full-time farmers	27	bus owner and driver	1
bauxite employees	10	butcher	1
shopkeepers	6	gas station franchise owner	1
old and don't work	5	hotel dishwasher	1
prison warders	5	mechanic at sugar estate	1
tailors	4	minister of religion	1
carpenters	4	newspaper peddler	1
employees at lime factory	4	painter	1
bakery employees	3	penner [a]	1
accountant	1	quarry	1
assistant bailiff	1	truck driver	1
bank clerk	1		
		Total: 82	

B. *Men who engage in one of the above occupations may also fall in one or more of the following four categories:*

men who hired out their labor to other farmers in Coco Hill within past five years	25
men who worked on road repairs within past five years	11
men who went to the United States on the farm contract within past five years	2
men who worked at a sugar estate within past five years	2

[a] A penner cares for cattle on a cattle property.

TABLE II

OCCUPATIONS OF ADULT FEMALES OF PERCY ROAD

housekeepers and some farming	24	mentally ill	2
full-time housekeepers	12	post office clerks	2
full-time farmers	10	bar tender	1
domestics	10	cook at hotel	1
old and no longer work	9	drug dispenser	1
shopkeepers	8	midwife	1
higglers	7	newspaper vender	1
teachers	7	street sweeper	1
seamstresses	3		
clerks	2	Total: 102	

TABLE III

AMOUNT OF LAND OWNED BY FARMERS ON PERCY ROAD [a]

Land	Adult Males (Percentage)
no land [b]	14
1 square to less than 3 acres	60
3 acres to less than 5 acres	14
5 acres to less than 10 acres	7
10 acres to less than 15 acres	4
more than 15 acres	1
Total	(59)

[a] Many of these farmers have supplementary occupations.
[b] These men do not own any land, but rent a small plot and/or work out as agricultural laborers.

TABLE IV

RELATIONSHIP BETWEEN OCCUPATION AND LAND OWNERSHIP
OF MALE HOUSEHOLD HEAD AND CHILDREN'S EDUCATIONAL
ATTAINMENT: PERCY ROAD

	Occupation			
	Full-Time Farmer		Farming and Other Occupation	
Land Ownership	less than 3 acres	more than 3 acres	less than 3 acres	more than 3 acres
children's education	%	%	%	%
post-primary school [a]	9	66	64	100
primary school or less	91	34	36	0
Total [b]	(11)	(6)	(14)	(8)

[a] At least one child has had post-primary school training in the past five years.
[b] Total number of households with children old enough to be attending/have attended post-primary school in the past five years.

Index

Agricultural Marketing Corporation, 5, 21
All-Island Banana Growers' Association, 25, 115, 121
Anglican Church, 25, 56, 57, 116
Apter, David, quoted, 148
Arawak Indians, 147

Banana Board, 12
banana industry, 4, 7, 22
Baptist Church, 25, 26, 38n., 73 and n., 74n.
bauxite industry, 4, 5, 6, 12, 49, 53, 70, 150
Bendix, Reinhard, 149
benefits from political parties, Coco Hill attitudes toward, 129–31
Bogle, Paul, 108n.
Braithwaite, Lloyd, 31n., 43n.
Bryce-Laporte, R. S., 32n.
Burial Scheme Hall (Coco Hill), 56
Bustamante, Alexander, 110, 111, 113n., 115, 128n.
Bustamante Industrial Trade Union, 111, 112, 113 and n.

Canada, Jamaicans in, 13, 64, 142, 151
Cane Road, 7, 8, 9, 14, 28, 114, 115, 120, 130, 136–39 passim; and Coco Hill, political differences between, 136–39, 140
cattle raising, 3, 7
Central America, Jamaicans in, 13, 109n.
child-centeredness, and education, 60–65
Christmas work (Coco Hill), 129 and n.
Church of God, 25, 26, 73, 74, 76, 93, 101

Coco Hill, 3, 4, 6, 8–10, 141; agricultural practices in, 6, 7; and Cane Road, political differences between, 136–39, 140; as changing community, 10–17; child-centeredness in, 60–65; Christmas work in, 129 and n.; churches in, 25, 26, 56, 73–77, 101–03; crops grown in, 7; disputes in, see disputes (Coco Hill); and education, see education; electrical facilities in, 14; entrepreneurs in, 20 and n., 22, 24, 25, 28, 74, 78; estate owners in, 20 and n., 22, 25, 28; farmers in, see farmers (Coco Hill); farming methods in, 6, 7; government services in, 12, 20; Head Teacher in, 53, 56 and n., 81, 82; health clinic in, 15, 139; higglers in, 20 and n., 21, 67; industrial development of, 12; and Jamaican government, attitudes toward, 125–28; Justices of the Peace in, 26–27; land ownership in, 6, 20, 21–22, 67, 68; leadership in, 25–27, 56n.; library in, 139; life styles in, 20, 22–25; mens' work in, 29; newspapers distributed in, 15; police records in, 64n.; police station in, 14, 139; political organization in, 114–40 passim; political patronage in, 118–20; population of, 3; postal facilities in, 14; prison in, 15–16; radio sets in, 14, 15; shops in, 15; soil types in, 7; status differentiation in, see status differentiation (Coco Hill); supermarket in, 15 and n.; television sets in, 14, 24; temperatures in, 7; transportation for,